WHISTLEBLOWER
IN PARIS

LEON R. KOZIOL

authorHOUSE®

AuthorHouse™
1663 Liberty Drive
Bloomington, IN 47403
www.authorhouse.com
Phone: 833-262-8899

Published by AuthorHouse 01/26/2022

ISBN: 978-1-6655-3240-2 (sc)
ISBN: 978-1-6655-3241-9 (hc)
ISBN: 978-1-6655-3239-6 (e)

Library of Congress Control Number: 2021914679

Print information available on the last page.

ABOUT THE AUTHOR

Dr. Leon Koziol is a human rights advocate who practiced law in federal and state courts. After earning his Juris Doctor degree in 1985, he dedicated the next thirty-five years to securing justice for diverse victims. His successes included jury verdicts, substantial recoveries, and precedent opinions. In 2004, he obtained a judgment invalidating the largest casino compact in New York. He also earned appearances on 60 Minutes, front page of the New York Times and other media.

In 2010, Leon took a conscientious stand against his profession for its abuse of parents in divorce and family courts. A victim himself, he soon exposed misconduct among jurists, lawyers and service providers who were promoting needless conflict for profit. Severe harm to children was treated as collateral damage. Incredible retributions followed, but the seizures of professional licenses, income capacities and father-daughter relations only increased his resolve for justice.

Nationwide efforts then expanded to include lobby initiatives, speaking events, a march down Pennsylvania Avenue under police escort, and a vigil at the Capitol for the lives lost to a corrupt system. All were ignored, adding support for George Floyd activists who declared that peaceful protest was ineffective. It also lent substance to a tactic of killing the messenger in the form of a "shoot on sight" warrant for child support and a survival mission that nearly cost Leon his life.

The shocking story which follows is a testament for whistleblower protection everywhere.

CONTENTS

**This Human Rights Odyssey
is based on a true story**

CHAPTER ONE

RETURN TO PARIS

Cumulous clouds were advancing toward the Maginot Line as our jet engines announced their approach to Charles de Gaulle Airport. Out of curiosity, I squinted eastward toward those extensive fortifications during another swing over Paris.

Somewhere out there was a barn where my father had been concealed when that Line proved ineffectual to Hitler's invasion. Somewhere out there my dad was returned to the war against the Nazis during the liberation of France.

His name was Louis, and after that war he wanted no more of the horrors he had survived in Europe. He ended up raising a family in the United States, land of liberty as he loved to call it, never imagining that his son would one day return here to escape persecution in America.

That may seem implausible to you, but it was occurring on this very flight. I'll explain as we go along. For now, it's the paradox of my incredible journey through a lucrative court system, a conscientious stand against my profession, and an evil that has lurked there for too long.

As I peered out the fuselage, thoughts of my predicament overshadowed the grandeur of the city below. Still incomprehensible was my pending status as a fugitive from justice, or more precisely a victim of injustice, a whistleblower not unlike Edward Snowden or Julian Assange. The main difference is that I hadn't even been accused of any crime. I was no threat to national security.

As remarkable as that paradox in the clouds, my only crime was that I wanted to spend more time with my precious daughters during a divorce case. While committing that crime, I was forced to expose the real ones in a government industry that was extinguishing parenthood. The shocking proof you will now discover provides convincing detail on how this is happening.

My ordeal was an ongoing one from the time I announced my stand at a news conference in 2010. Most victims of retaliation could withstand a demotion, job termination, adverse publicity, harm to family members, or even a public beating by errant police officers. But my case had all these combined, and much more, a perfect storm of sorts that first hit the radar in 2008.

Its perpetrators figured that no human could sustain such abuse for so long. Who would believe it anyway? Like Nazis in the day, they subjected me to false charges, star chamber inquisitions, seizure of my children, ruination of my livelihood, and an endless array of government targeting. They even took aim at my life when their tactics failed to end my crusade against corruption.

It's not like they all planned it out in some clandestine room, but my alarming exposures had the natural effect of inducing joint retaliation in the age of internet. Ultimately, I would vanish with my judicial whistleblowing. Judicial waterboarding is the way I put it before the Supreme Court. But for that court to hear my ordeal was to invite an indictment of an entire state court system, and its members had not yet shown the courage to distinguish themselves for the history books.

It brought to mind the five years my dad endured in a Nazi concentration camp after his capture on the eastern front. His stories included urine slurped from the floor and firearms put in his face to pattern Russian Roulette. Dodging the fate of others, he was not among the three Koziols memorialized at Auchwitz. I learned of them from my sister after a retreat she made to Poland.

So if he could survive all that fighting a much larger regime, my persecution should be a walk in the park. No doubt genetics were a major factor so far: gang fights during boyhood, high school football when corporal punishment was standard, legal hazing in my college fraternity, law school in Chicago, a death-defying event on a mountain and, of course, the presidential elections.

But with all the trappings of a Dixie lynching, my divorce was turned into a calamity of shocking proportion. I never imagined my free speech would trigger such oppression in my homeland to compel a petition before the United Nations, resistance to a support warrant in Lake Placid, an alert before national media at a murder scene in South Carolina, and flight to a Pacific island.

I was not on some honeymoon. I had already done that in Paris. If only I could reverse the clock of time. But a prominent black minister in Manhattan declared this to be my destiny. So here I was, whatever he meant, and it did turn up corruption that would make John Grisham ecstatic. If there was a destiny, it was shared by every mom and dad since the beginning of humanity itself.

For all the injury I sustained, this could have been the challenge of a lifetime. But I had stirred a hornets' nest, exposing the raw underbelly of a child control syndicate, a judicial forum where countless parents were summoned to resolve sensitive family matters only to be treated like common criminals. Such arguments were offered again before our high court in 2016 where I sought in vain to secure fair access and a novel opinion supporting an expansion of its number.[1]

An accomplished civil rights lawyer, I was naturally drawn to challenge the heartless seizure of children in our third branch of government. That's the better description of divorce court. Family court was its evil child where the real carnage occurred. After a two year separation without incident, everything was promising for my daughters. That's when an invasion was launched by judges and lawyers anxious to conquer my world in a parenting environment they did not belong.

A Supreme Court justice had this to say about America's family courts: "Under our Constitution, the condition of being a boy does not justify a kangaroo court." [2] But that was 1967. An erosion of rights since then has changed his pronouncement to the condition of being a father or career mom separated from offspring under the stigmatizing classification of "non-custodial parent."

Meanwhile the national focus remains on parent-child separations among illegals at our borders.

Is the disregard of our own crisis then explained by a blind surrender of rights? The answer remains censored by propaganda. The state dictates to the parents that it is acting in the *best interests of the child*, a dubious claim before it bankrupts them in a protracted legal battle. It manufactures an incendiary contest over one's offspring reminiscent

---

[1] Koziol v King, Supreme Court Docket No. 16-512, October 17, 2016. This petition sought a declaration of the court's growing incapacity to hear cases commensurate with a vast increase in population. Five years later, a group of congress members sought a similar expansion focused more on politics than merit. The Koziol petition was therefore offered as an option for President Joe Biden's commission to study Supreme Court overhauls.

[2] In re Gault, 387 US 1 at pg. 28.

of the Roman Coliseum only to reap huge profits from the crimes and emotional trauma which predictably result.

Victims who oppose this centralized power face the prospect of losing everything in these courts. And the retaliation occurs without due process, jury rights, or other constitutional protections. [3] It's all justified by "the law" created by those who crave that power. During my reform efforts across the country, I encountered victims who could not fathom what was truly happening to them while being subjected to undue scrutiny and evaluations for every kind of indiscretion.

This easily abused *best interests of the child* standard remains the weapon to achieve all sorts of unconscionable outcomes. Many children are effectively controlling their parents under this system, an inverted order of childrearing as I described it in my reports. Moms and dads under constant threat of losing "custody" are spoiling these children while surrendering their natural authority to "birthing" concoctions and those more focused on self-love than time tested honors.

---

[3] In his 550 page book, The New Whistleblower's Handbook (2017) at xvi, leading whistleblower attorney, Stephen Martin Kohn, depicts the realities of retaliation:

Difficult choices face (those) who uncover wrongdoing. According to a study published in the *New England Journal of Medicine,* even whistleblowers who won their cases had a most difficult time, both at work and at home. While fighting their cases, they suffered "devastating financial consequences," including (the forced sale of) their homes, having their cars repossessed, and losing their retirement accounts. Many whistleblowers simply reported that they had "lost everything."

That handbook was obtained from its author during a 2017 Annual Whistleblower Convention in Washington D.C. Although the ordeals documented there are alarming, none rise to the level endured here by a whistleblower exposing the wrongs committed by those who preside over such cases. It is a niche few lawyers dare occupy. See also, Turner v Rogers, 564 US 431 (2011)(due process and counsel denied to support defendant after jail term)

That was the essence of my public message. It was certainly not novel but promoted by a lawyer and parent singularly qualified to expose it. The abused power I was after had its roots in feudal England where the King declared his sovereignty over all children. That edict was adopted by the courts here despite its clash with our Constitution. [4] It gives pause to reflect on a state leader who understood this power and exploited it over time to wage the most horrific war in human history:

The state must declare the child to be the most precious treasure of the people. As long as the government is perceived as working for the benefit of children, the people will happily endure almost any curtailment of liberty ...

Adolph Hitler, *Mein Kampf,* Publ. Houghton Miflin, 1943, pg. 403.

With little notice, these courts have morphed into a custody war machine for revenue and fee purposes, pitting state against parents. This feudal fiction has been abused well beyond the limited purpose of family courts. They are now monitoring every aspect of our lives using power that would be the envy of the NSA, CIA and IRS. To be sure, a veteran judge condemned this evil long ago. Judge Dennis Duggan bucked his judiciary by refusing continued use of degrading terms such as "custody" and "visitation." [5] Here's how he justified his revolt against the state:

> At the outset, the Court notes that the terms 'custody' and 'visitation' have outlived their usefulness. Indeed their use tends to place any discussion and allocation of family rights into an oppositional framework. 'Fighting for custody' directs the process towards determining winners and losers. The children, always in the middle, usually turn out to be the losers...

---

[4] Finlay v Finlay, 240 NY 429, 148 NE 625 (1925), quoting In re Spence, 41 Eng. Rep. 937 (1847)

[5] Webster v Ryan, 729 NYS2d 315 (Albany Fam. Ct. 2001) at Fn. 1.

> *This Court has abandoned the use of the word 'visitation' in its Orders, using the phrase 'parenting time' instead. If the word 'custody' did not so permeate our statutes and was not so ingrained into our psyches, that word would be the next to go… This misplaced focus draws parents into contention and conflict, drawing the worst from them at a time when their children need their parents' best.*

Duggan evaded the core problem in his decision, that elephant in the courtroom known as profit motive. Still, he was precipitously close to triggering vital reforms. It was no surprise then that his decision was quickly reversed on appeal, and despite similar condemnations in a 2006 judicial report, [6] the inflammatory depictions of mom and dad have survived. In my own reports, I urged that such terms were more appropriate for prisons and funerals, not a forum known as family court.

Our federal government remains a major cause. Its bureaucrats have become the super-parent of society through coercive funding laws. Enamored with wars declared on any issue to incite tax hikes, they managed to convert sensitive family disputes into rewarding public battlegrounds with collateral damage to our economy through declines in productivity. Family judges became so overwhelmed they delegated their entrusted duties to outsiders who complicated ready solutions.

My credible reform message threatened this gold mine. It was one that might take flight with social and secondary media. Hence it had to be exterminated at its inception. Suddenly I was a one-man fighting machine according to a talk show host in Florida. I had silent supporters, parents and concerned citizens who could navigate beyond the propaganda of a self-regulating court system. But they were

---

[6] 2006 New York Matrimonial Commission Report to the Chief Justice (the "Miller Report").

intimidated, and this was also a prophesy of sorts which made me more of a nemesis.

During my reform crusade, I explained how power brokers were laying a foundation for the New World Order through this custody institution. Orchestrated court conflict was being exploited to show parental incompetence for an eventual state take-over of childrearing. It was following the lead of compulsory education and how that became institutionalized.

Judicial targeting began with family court beneficiaries. Divorce lawyers, child attorneys, diverse psychologists, case evaluators and forensic experts were only some of the ones I extolled as court predators. They were the lemmings exacerbating an epidemic. It was the Goliath I was out to slay.

Unrealistic perhaps, but there were weapons in my own arsenal. I had a stellar professional record, won substantial recoveries,[7] defeated high profile law firms to invalidate the most lucrative casino in New York,[8] set free speech precedent as a city corporation counsel,[9] New York Times sent reporters to my law office to cover my campaign for Congress,[10] and Morley Safer did the same for a feature on 60 Minutes.[11] How could they discredit all that and more? Well they did.

Still, someone had to make this stand for our children and future generations. It is said that a hearse comes with no trailer hitch. You can't

[7] Patterson v City of Utica, 370 F.3d 322 (2nd Cir. 2004)($333,820 verdict argued before Justice Sonia Sotomayor)

[8] Oneida Nation v Oneida County, 132 F. Supp.2d 71 (NDNY 2000); Peterman v Pataki, 2004 NY Slip Op 51092

[9] Koziol v Hanna, 107 F. Supp. 2d 170 (2000)(city gag order challenged to successful jury verdict in federal court)

[10] Jonathan Hicks, *A House Seat Won by Republicans Since 1950 Is Now in Play*, nytimes.com, April 2, 2006

[11] Morley Safer, *Whose land is it anyway?* CBS 60 Minutes, Sunday, May 23, 1999

take your belongings to an afterlife. In this cause, I had found my life's purpose, a way of helping people long after my time on earth was over. Everything in my being had finally come together. Every child in every location was now my moral client.

But Goliath was a trillion-dollar industry. It first impacted me through a judge who refused to hear my arguments against the antiquated entitlements of Title IV-D of the Social Security Act. In lay terms, this was the Child Support Standards Act which required the naming of a "Custodial Parent" for state courts to earn federal funds.[12] It became a CP factory with little faith in parent cooperation.

Couldn't anyone else see the pollution billowing out of those judicial smokestacks? With so much focus on global warming, homeland security and industrial waste, how could lawmakers glide so casually over an "inconvenient truth" at the root of so many other societal problems? With more than 300,000 lawyers in New York and California alone, this pollution was growing by the day.

A precedent ruling was therefore crucial, but my divorce judge was nearing retirement while mired in the stereotypes of a distant past when moms stayed home and dads worked to support children. He would shoe-horn me into that inferior non-custodial classification and presume that anything else I did was irresponsible. That's before he was replaced by a record forty trial level jurists.

Due to my long public history in our judicial district, impartiality here was suspect, requiring a venue change. But contrary to logic, my motion for that change was denied in 2007, leaving me with no choice but to move for recusal (disqualification) of each assigned judge. Many stepped down of their own accord due to personal interactions, adding to the wisdom of that motion.

---

[12] Bast v Rossoff, 91 NY2d 723 (1998); Dept of Family v DHHS of U.S., 588 F.3d 740 (1st Cir. 2009)

However, the clear error on that denial had far greater implications. Each judge assignment delayed a final outcome. And as we all know, justice delayed is justice denied. This did not seem to bother these gurus in robes as they continued to debate behind closed doors who might finally be able to judge my case. But my daughters were maturing by the minute. We simply could wait no longer. So I filed in federal court. To my added detriment, this meant I had to name judges as defendants.

But to access that court, I had to overcome the state's sovereign immunity. For precedent purposes, this required the naming of every party who had impaired my parenting time or liberty rights in their personal and official capacities.[13] As the retributions escalated, so did the number of actions I was forced to bring. This persisted for years featuring one 45-page decision that disposed of more than 30 prominent defendants. [14] For an originally uncontested divorce, it was a read to behold.

As reflected by that decision, the sheer number of invaders upon my parenting world was proof enough of corruption per se. On the sadistic side, I was being defamed, faulted, and punished for complying with laws upon laws. Sadly, but predictably over time, all relief was denied in federal court, thereby reverting me to state court where prejudice was now rampant. There I continued to urge that fathers remained a last bastion of institutional discrimination due to the custody mandate.

Shared parenting was a preferred model, but my divorce judge was not about to risk his reputation to do the right thing. Instead, he punted, referring me to the legislature for reform. Hence, you might say

---

[13] Ex Parte Young, 209 US 123 (1923)(competing interests of the 11th and 14th Amendments required treatment of persons violating the latter to be outside the scope of the former, considered by many critics to be a fiction); Troxel v Granville, 530 US 57 (2000)(parenting is "the oldest liberty interest protected by the Constitution")
[14] Parent v State, 786 F. Supp. 2d 516 (NDNY 2011)

this entire ordeal was court ordered. That I should single-handedly seek a judicial remedy in a legislative assembly was like having a mechanic repair a car in a stadium. Such lobbying would require a much greater level of critical public speech. Before a lawmaker could sponsor a reform bill, his constituency would need to be convinced that the old law was flawed.

When I aspired to do exactly that, it was the judiciary which opened fire on my speech rights in the forums where they were entitled to the greatest protection. [15] My exposure of such flaws outside the courthouse was evidently so offensive that a family judge threatened to remove me from "his" courthouse for making five objections during a custody hearing. When that failed to intimidate, he issued a gag order on my website that was removed after a challenge in New York Supreme Court.

A legislative approach was a herculean task, and my divorce judge knew it. Shared parenting bills had been routinely squashed by special interests and bar associations in states across the country. So, like the abortion right, I pursued the fast track through our courts, insisting quite logically that the much older parenting right which enhanced life deserved at least the same protection as the one which destroyed life without having to go before a gridlock legislature. [16]

New York was widely known to have the most dysfunctional

---

[15] On April 28, 2021, the Supreme Court heard arguments involving a 14-year old cheerleader disciplined for vulgar expression off campus directed at school officials, Mahanoy School District v B.L., Docket No. 20-255. Governed largely by 1969 precedent giving protection for student speech that was neither disruptive nor present on school grounds, the high court granted a petition to hear this case in contrast with those filed by this author to obtain whistleblower protection for attorney speech outside the courthouse that exposed judge corruption.

[16] Meyer v Nebraska, 262 US 390 (1923); Roe v Wade, 410 US 113 (1973)

legislature in America. [17] Reputable studies declared it, late budgets proved it, and politicians campaigned on that theme. One ethics commission after another was condemned as impotent. In 2013, I was invited to testify before the Moreland Commission on Public Corruption where I sought to dissolve the window-dressing Commission on Judicial Conduct. Instead, it was the Corruption Commission that was shut down.[18]

The futility of seeking a judicial remedy in our legislative branch was as obvious as the abortion bills were prior to *Roe v Wade*. No, this was not my Goliath. Such a deflection would not work on a lawyer who had held office in all three branches locally. Defamatory court decisions under the protection of judicial immunity would not dissuade me either. One useful way to relate my crusade is by quoting the late New York Senate Leader Joseph Bruno from his book, *Keep Swinging*. [19]

As one of the few survivors of federal criminal prosecutions against prominent state lawmakers, Joe chronicled thirty years of corruption, dysfunction, and budget impasses during his long tenure. These prosecutions cost state taxpayers many millions of dollars, demonstrating how politicians will spare no amount of other people's money to destroy

---

[17] Brennan Center for Justice at New York University School of Law, *The New York Legislative Process: An Analysis and Blueprint for reform* (2004); *Still Broken: New York State Legislative Reform* (2008)

[18] This commission was created by New York Governor Andrew Cuomo to address a "culture of corruption in Albany." However, when testimonials began to implicate the governor himself, the commission was prematurely closed in 2014. This incited one of the speakers, federal prosecutor Preet Bharara, to seize commission files resulting in convictions for the leaders of both houses of the legislature and a top Cuomo aide. The governor managed to evade similar liability but as fate would have it, he would later be subjected to multiple investigations for sexual harassment, family favoritism, abuse of state resources and falsified nursing home reports.

[19] Joseph Bruno, *Keep Swinging*, Post Hill Press, pg. 253 (2017)

an adversary. Here is what Joe concluded before his conviction was set aside due to intervening Supreme Court precedent:

> *You'd get no argument from me that the New York State Senate and Assembly were in dire need of ethics reform. Yet if the citizens… ever got around to demanding those changes, it would behoove the people to pay special attention to the behavior of prosecutors and judges who cared more about making a splash in the media than they did about justice.*

Well this book is about justice and that "special attention" from our citizenry, a collection of shocking stories which reduced a prominent lawyer and model parent into a bankrupt fugitive. It explains why Joe suffered as he did in court after remaining oblivious to all those citizens who complained before the very commissions he helped create. It details the potential consequences for those who truly care about abused children and seriously act to reform our courts.

It is also a story of love and devotion. You can send a man across the world, and he'll sacrifice his life in the war on terrorism. Cultivate violence through draconian laws or false charges, still he'll risk himself in the name of public safety. You can even revive debtor prisons under pretext of child support, and he'll do his time under protest. But never come between a daddy and his little girls. Even when they're ninety years of age, he's building mansions for them in heaven.

CHAPTER 2

OVERGROUND RAILROAD

I was not the only one drawn to the windows of our plane. Assorted reactions could be heard to the Eiffel Tower and various palatial structures as they came into view with each stage of our descent. Judging by the excitement, most passengers were tourists.

Two couples were on their honeymoon, a group of Brooklyn teachers were here for an international conference of some kind, and a dad was regularly attending to an infant next to me. We talked intermittently, and I hardly heard a peep from the little one during our long flight. That allowed me to get some shut-eye. I wanted to commend his "parenting skills" as we arrived at the terminal, but he needed no patronizing, so I passed on it.

Inside, sunlight was radiating from giant picture windows. For me, it was more of a florescent glow. I was burdened by the thought of never seeing home or my girls again. It reminded me of a solar eclipse, the only one I had ever experienced outside my law office years earlier.

My displaced condition soon eclipsed those thoughts. I had made it through customs before an arrest warrant could be issued for a debt euphemistically termed *child support*. That warrant was expected any day now and the way they were being enforced, it brought new meaning to the word draconian. A dad could be imprisoned indefinitely through recurring delinquencies. A mere relocation over state lines with a $5,000 arrearage could result in a felony conviction.

Adding to that the status of judicial whistleblower and a perfect storm was born in my case. Child support was one of many pretexts used to censor my public criticisms. My persecutors had seized all my realistic means for earning income, from an indefinite suspension of my law and driver's licenses to seizure of my assets and reputation needed for alternate employment.

Meanwhile my obligations remained at fixed levels based on earnings recorded prior to closure of my law practice. Now, many years later, I could not even maintain a bank account for alternate business operations. It became a form of house arrest morphing into homelessness and a debt well beyond any chance of satisfaction. Interest and penalties were growing by the day with no bankruptcy option or judicial protection for basic liberties under our Bill of Rights.

It gave the state everything it needed to eliminate me through violent methods, if necessary, and given my decades of civil rights litigation, that could mean serious injury or even death behind bars. It was either fold or flight, a scene right out of the former Soviet Union, reminiscent of Aleksandr Solzhenitsyn or Attorney Chen Guangcheng, a 2012 exile of Communist China.

I had sympathizers. Dr. Joseph Sorge was one of them. Founder of Divorce Corp, a public interest group focused on reforming the divorce industry, he contributed millions of dollars to change America for the better. He even produced a documentary for theatres around the country while tracking down parent advocates, child experts and lawyers like me to join the cause.

I was referred to him by internet sentries, those Paul Reveres of the parenting revolution who collaborated to bring allies together. Utterly outgunned, they were like the underground in the Terminator movie. Joe produced a mini-documentary of my crusade to repeal Title IV-D funding and the incentivized conflict it brought to family courts. During my seclusion in Paris, we shared our progress and strategies by phone as he investigated divorce models in other parts of Europe.

My ethics monitors were infuriated by all this, exploiting Joe's use of the innocuous words "civil rights attorney" as a violation of a law license suspension order. They filed inquiries against me which had the effect of further chilling my public statements. Verily, they were doing everything in their power to discredit me through my learned status. No one in their right mind could conclude that I was rendering legal advice to thousands of viral viewers I would never meet.

Joe was aware of the suspension order but under no obligation to comply. In sharp contrast, a Syracuse newspaper printed a similar attorney reference in an article headline weeks later. It featured federal judge (and gene theorist) Gary Sharpe who was simply *considering* a ban on my civil rights filings.[20] There were no similar inquiries, leading one to conclude that any kind of reputation harm leaked to major media would be favored over positive events in other outlets.

I survived the inquiries but only after obtaining court permission to make the witch hunt public during a confidential disciplinary process and allowing Divorce Corp to film the ethics hearing that resulted. More on the startling aspects of that later, but the inquiries were enough

---

[20] John O'Brien, *Federal judge plans to ban Utica lawyer from filing lawsuits*, Syracuse. com, August 27, 2015; See also Benjamin Weiser, *Court Rejects Judge's Assertion of a Child Pornography Gene,* NY Times.com, January 28, 2011; United States v Cossey, 632 F.3d 82 (2nd Cir. 2011)(Gary Sharpe removed from case by federal appeals court due to gene theory that "seriously affects fairness, integrity, and public reputation of judicial proceedings.")

to dissuade me from speaking at a family law reform conference Joe had sponsored near our nation's capital.

My ordeal was needlessly complicated for revenge and then blamed on me to scare away public oversight. Crafty jurists would use terms such as "rambling" and "incomprehensible" to derail my logical arguments against a lucrative custody institution that was creating monsters among our offspring and crimes of unimaginable proportion. Remarkably, the intellectual guardians of our First Amendment marched over my logic like zombies in an Independence Day parade.

Simply put, judges were abusing their powers to kill a reform message that applied to their own misconduct. While approving large scale verdicts for civil rights victims against employers and law enforcement, they were using their own guns to kill a similar victim. I likened it to a Rodney King beating with the fists and batons replaced by orders and edicts, a hypocrisy of monumental proportion. They twisted every fact and precedent in a light most damaging to their public critic.

How could I explain any of this to lay persons at Joe's reform conference across the Potomac? Attended by unofficial reform delegates from most of our fifty states, it was a resounding success by any prior standard. But upon conclusion, mainstream media treated it as a large scale gripe session by losers in divorce or family court. Any positive outcome remains to be seen, but one thing it did yield, a standing ovation that put wind in my sails needed for my overseas flight.

Another sympathizer was Anthony Pappas of St. John's University. Armed with a Ph.D. from Yale and another degree from MIT, he was doggedly committed to ending judicial immunity. As will be shown, his drive was well placed given the millions of dollars he spent in fees during a protracted divorce without child issue. A finance professor, he raised funds behind this daring mission in Paris. Left unanswered now was the means for self-support into my unforeseen future.

No one exiting the jet bridge seemed interested in any diversions. I was not in any such rush. I had hardly slept in days. A basic shave, cleaning and shedding of formal attire would improve my chances of anonymity on the streets. But there was a more ominous reason. I had no place to go. I was literally without a host or appointment anywhere. And I was all alone.

I pondered how those slaves must have felt while traveling the Underground Railroad. Professor Pappas described his version as the Overground Railroad. He was adamant about saving me from tyrants he knew all too well. "Judicial bullies," he called them in his writings. As for me, I wasn't sure what to call this, an escape to freedom or a further descent into refugee status.

Unlike victims of domestic violence and child abduction, there was no established network for aiding victims of child support abuse. After so many years in the parent rights movement I could only discern a collection of keyboard warriors, few committed protesters, and no lobbying group. Gender discrimination was routinely overlooked, and whistleblowers were made to appear crazy.

In my experience with divorce victims, growing numbers have been subjected to psychiatric evaluations on the slightest allegations of a scorned ex-spouse or tactic-minded lawyer. The psychiatrist, employed by the court, had little or no confidentiality duties to a non-patient, just another protected anomaly of a sick system that few knew about until it was too late.

In the end, parents rightfully stressed over the threat of losing their children in a custody battle, or debtor imprisonment for child support, would be made to believe they were basket cases. If the parent was a father, his condition might be nothing more than resistance to a justice system sworn to equality which still discriminates on account of sex. In my reports and court filings, I compared it to the anger issues of slaves opposed to their condition prior to the Civil War.

The scam here went something like this: parents were incompetent to challenge legal matters especially without counsel when their means dry up. Self-represented lawyers were incompetent for a different reason. Emotional attachments impaired their judgments. But the same labels were often seized upon to reach a more stigmatizing level when a target parent could be accused of some made-up psychological disorder. This then justified a judge referral for expert evaluations.

By the time the system was done protecting itself, any whistleblower could be dispensed as a nut case to any media inquirer or oversight investigator. Even the conforming parent trusting a judge referral order could end up with an outrageous report laced with inflammatory detail, rapid fire torture to incite a violent reaction. Accurately put, it was more proof of deranged justice, voodoo therapy for court created chaos having a ready cure at any local bar, coffee shop or fitness center.

These particular court predators would issue all sorts of alarming reports to fill their egos while currying favor with their judge employers. There are literally hundreds of disorders and abject conditions in the DSM manuals issued over the years for insurance coverage. Most, if not all of them, are subjective, encompassing every kind of human behavior, and the only one not defined is normalcy. Every lawyer and judge I ever knew could be diagnosed under the latest manual. [21]

Indeed, the judge and his expert may be more pressing candidates for therapy given their callous indifference to this epidemic. During my practice, I pleasantly came across professionals who refused to accept court assignments due to the aggravated harm they inflicted. The drug

---

[21] "The new edition of the DSM 'bible' is so flawed that the U.S. National Institute of Mental Health is right to abandon it," eminent psychiatrist, Allen Frances, New Scientist, May 15, 2013

industry could easily be the most unconscionable predator hunting down a ready flow of addicts. Medical doctors also weighed in with cancer and other treatments to unleash a tornado of fleecing.

This involuntary referral practice has virtually no accountability. Some beneficiaries might even argue that a normal report rises to a level of contempt. After all, if a judge orders an evaluation, there must be a problem even when he or she knows little about psychology, medicine, parenting or, in Sharpe's case, genetics. This is not to say that all evaluations should be nixed, but the broad discretion for ordering them is easily abused for ulterior purposes and rarely questioned.

Okay, so my rage against the machine is getting obvious. When your precious little ones are at stake, it can do that to you. In any event, I needed major overhauls. So off I went to the nearest rest room shared by a few stragglers with similar goals. Even there I could get no reprieve. As I gazed into the mirror, I took note of the pain in my reflection, the bottom line of sleepless nights, the whereabouts of my girls, and the contempt I felt for those perpetrating this horrific scam.

I thought about the dead and walking dead, victims of murder, suicide, premature death and those awaiting justice that would never come. I thought about Investigator Joe Longo, a father of four so traumatized after support court that he used a common kitchen knife to leave them with no parents for life.[22] The predators just kept pounding him with confiscated weapons, protection orders, support intercepts and career damage without considering any breaking points.

I thought about Thomas Ball, product of an overzealous child protection agency who sat down one day on the steps of a New Hampshire courthouse to protest family court abuse. [23] But this was no sit-in, no *occupy court* mission. He poured gas over his head and burned

---

[22] <u>Pearce v Longo</u>, 766 F. Supp.2d 367 (NDNY 2011)

[23] Mark Arsenault, *Dad leaves clues to his desperation*, boston.com, July 10, 2011

himself alive. I cringed at the extreme pain he must have suffered before and during this holocaust. In the end, there was no national coverage, no court reforms, they merely washed his ashes into the sewer.

I thought about Alec Baldwin, one of the few victims who did attract national coverage. During his high profile divorce with Kim Bassinger, he dutifully complied with forensic evaluation orders, hoping to quickly exit this matrix as he described it. However, protracted deliberations in California's court system forced him to expose dysfunction among judges, lawyers, evaluators and others. His goal ultimately was to prevent unsuspecting parents from becoming victims. But in the end, he nearly became the ultimate victim. His own words have long been forgotten:

> *My family and closest friends were still there for me, but even some of them had grown perplexed by and weary of the assault on my parental rights that seemed to have no end. On the deepest level, my situation now seemed hopeless to me as well. I had gone to sleep many nights doubting that I had the desire to face these problems another day... Driving up the Taconic Parkway, heading to an inn in the Berkshire Mountains, I began to think about what little known town I would repair to in order to commit suicide. What semi-remote Massachusetts state park could I hike deep into and shoot myself? What bed-and-breakfast could I check into and overdose there? On Long Island, I thought about the old Jeep I owned and the emissions it gave off. When I returned to New York, the thought of jumping out of the window of my apartment was with me every night for weeks.* [24]

I thought about so many victims I encountered during my crusade against this killing machine, a mom who drove her children into the Hudson River, the Iraq war veteran who attempted suicide only to be saved through my intervention, a member of our parenting rights organization who hung himself from a tree in his back yard, the mom

---

[24] Alec Baldwin, *A Promise to Ourselves*, St. Martin's Press, at pg. 183 (2008)

who called me daily for help until vanishing altogether, and the dad I dissuaded from a kidnapping of his own children now hiding in Israel.

As I revisited the interview with that Florida talk show host, an aggrieved dad who took his life a few years later, the roar of a jet engine shook me from my daze. I collected my toiletries and rushed for the baggage terminal. I had all of my vital possessions that could be carried in two heavy traveling bags, and the last thing I needed was to have them disappear at this moment.

Now that I had finally arrived, I began to ask myself whether I made the right decision to come here. But given the resourcefulness of the people I met along this Overground Railroad, I was confident that I could slip away undetected to countless places. And if I was going to be apprehended, it would occur in an exotic place with a more inviting climate.

At the baggage conveyor, I took note of a couple with two little girls still waiting for their possessions. They looked a lot like mine did when I flew them to Disney World. It brought a smile to my face as I imagined them with me here at this very moment. During our recent years apart, it's as if they were popping up everywhere with constant reminders of my greater mission.

CHAPTER 3

RELIGION UNDER SIEGE

I left the terminal with my crucial life possessions, laptop, electronic devices and modern weaponry intended to wage war in exile against this dysfunctional court system in my homeland. I hopped onto an airport shuttle after lugging my bags up the steps with all I could do to get situated. Then I sat back to take in the scenery, eager to focus my mind on anything but my plight. The first stop was well into the city along the expressway from the north. I would switch over to cab service at the Madeleine much closer to my destination to save on costs, as much as seventy euros or $100 at unofficial exchange rates.

My destination was the 18th Arrondissement, one of the city's twenty districts, better known as Montmartre. Essentially a hill community situated on the Rive Droite or Right Bank of the Seine River, it boasted the highest point in Paris topped by the magnificent Sacre Coeur (Sacred Heart) Basilica. From its steps, the panoramic view was spectacular.

I had booked an economy room on Rue Ordener along the back side of the hill strategically located near the central precinct station. This is where asylum applications were initiated for this district. Everything in my world now was tenuous, and if word from home included a formally issued child support warrant, I would then make my move.

For now, I was good. The north side was populated predominantly by locals and immigrants from former French colonies, Algeria being one that seemed to stand out by conversations I overheard. Always on foot or subway, the chances of finding me here were quite remote with my i-phone treated with great caution. My passport had survived customs and I would spend the rest of my life here rather than any time in an American prison for exercising my God-given rights.

The Basilica had a religious appeal for me, almost as if it would offer me a cloak of protection high above my hotel. After registering and settling in, it was the first place I visited. I had been to Paris only one other time, and that was many years ago during my honeymoon. We had so many sites on our itinerary that we could not get to this one. Sacred Heart had a main cathedral with a chapel for more private worship on its lower west side. That chapel became my sanctuary.

Typically, a line of people prevented efficient access at the front entrance so I would spend my time as a local might in the less crowded compartment of the Basilica. I came here almost daily, usually in the afternoon or evening before wandering off among the nearby streets of an eclectic artsy district where outdoor entertainment gave added appeal. The hill was also ideal for a workout routine culminating on the arduous flights of stairs leading to the top at Rue Foyatier.

Sharpton, Forbes and Father Karloutsos

Professor Pappas would have been pleased with my routine. Victim of a divorce still ongoing for nearly two decades, he was raked over the coals financially, emotionally, and professionally. He had spent over $2 million in diverse fees to defend against fabricated charges when grounds were still mandated. A decree was finally granted after a jury trial on those grounds, but the next phase featured a protracted battle over asset distribution, the price paid for a long term marriage.

Like me, Tony was religious and principled. It was therefore inevitable that he would get caught up in the reform movement. It's how we met. Tony was also deeply committed to his ancestry. A contributor to the Greek Orthodox Diocese of New York, he took me to see his pastor at the Archbishop rectory near Central Park, convinced that we had to get clergy involved.

There we met Father Alex Karloutsos, a highly regarded cleric and power broker of sorts. He offered to share my reports with media contacts and members of the Trump administration. Only weeks later, there he was on the news during an event at the White House before disappearing with the president in some other room. He also had proven affiliations with the Biden family.

During another meeting on the day of my departure from JFK, Reverend James Forbes, retired pastor of Riverside Church in Manhattan, joined us. He was over eighty years of age at the time with a distinguished history as a top African-American cleric. Father Alex startled us with an opening reference to Reverend Al Sharpton and how wrongly accused prosecutor, Steve Pagones, never got his redemption after the Tawana Brawley scandal during the late 1980s.

I was side-tracked but veritably impressed by this cleric's dedication to his flock three decades later. Mr. Pagones had been accused in an alleged rape and racist beating of a fifteen year old. A Grand Jury eventually concluded that the story was made up. In a defamation lawsuit that took ten years to conclude, another jury found Sharpton and various co-defendants liable for their accusations, but Pagones never recovered all the money damages that were assessed. [25]

---

[25] Frank Bruni, *Finally, His Day in Court; Man Wrongly Accused in Brawley Case Will Be Heard*, The New York Times, March 15, 1998

I could relate to Mr. Pagones because I was also falsely accused during my divorce as was Professor Pappas. All of the offense petitions filed against me over a ten-year period were thrown out with only one going to a hearing and no accountability regarding my accusers. I did my best to mediate the cleric dispute at the rectory, but in the end we all agreed that the divorce industry was our common target, an evil which was harming all religions.

Perhaps moved by my sacrifices or stand against my profession, Reverend Forbes offered to have a private lunch with me when we concluded. It's as if he sensed something after hearing my pitch to Father Alex. The criticism of Al Sharpton did not seem to ruffle Dr. James Forbes in the least as he shifted from cleric to civil rights advocate. We exited the rectory and got into a chat at the first diner we could find along Madison Avenue, a place called Nectar Coffee Shop.

There I spilled my guts.

"Reverend, why me? I mean what did I do to deserve all this? A model parent, accomplished civil right attorney, deeply spiritual, and I attend church services every Sunday. I've never even been accused of a crime. Help me understand what's happening. I want my life back."

"The answer may be that most lawyers today are set in their ways," he quickly responded. "They don't hear any spiritual calling because they're too obsessed with man's laws and not God's law. Do you really think you simply fell into this crusade, that you got a calling to be punished?"

"Well it sure feels that way, reverend, I lost everything and accomplished nothing."

"No sir, not true," he shot back with the first emotion I had detected in him all morning. "Just look at all the people you're saving, the inspiration and hope you're giving to so many. There's a greater meaning behind your skills now. Your life's no longer about money and routine."

"Then what is it about, a life in the streets with the homeless?"

"Not at all. God will provide for you as he is today with Tony's assistance. It's just that your purpose has not yet been revealed to you."

It's as if the cleric Forbes had returned, anxious to name another disciple for his own flock. He was that intense, studying my face for an honest reaction. I pondered his private sermon for a moment, one that was delivered with far better oratory than I could reproduce in any text. Professor Pappas was just now joining us at our table. Then I responded.

"Yeah, maybe, it's true that I saved a number of moms and dads from suicide. Still, here I am on the run from a child support warrant, so how am I good to anyone as a fugitive? I expect it will be issued sometime after a court hearing tomorrow, but I won't be at that hearing. I'll be seeking human rights protection in a foreign land."

"Can you believe what you're hearing, reverend?" Tony cut in. "This is a civil rights lawyer, he won big cases for the little guy. He lived by his oath and our Constitution. Now he's being pursued like an animal, persecuted for his beliefs. I'd call it a modern day crucifixion."

"I'll die in any jail cell, reverend, if I surrender to this persecution," I added, "maybe not bodily, but surely in spirit or in health with the real criminals in my midst. That's something my mind can't wrap around. Talk about cruel and unusual punishment. They've resurrected debtor prisons now. I can sympathize with Attorney Pagones, but at least he kept his family and freedoms."

The reverend winced. He then lunged into a sermon regarding my destiny, one that was not for me to understand or decline. As only he could explain it, tormented people like Tony were reliant on me to make a difference. I could not dispute his personalized rendition. Still, it did not allay my concerns. That day, Jim Forbes became my friend, a beacon of light on the dark seas.

Trifecta of Judicial Bullies

There were many cases of corruption I had been retained to investigate as a trial attorney. Tony's was off the charts. He was the divorce equivalent of a wrongfully convicted murderer yet to be released by the Innocence Project. He deserved a remedy to the injustices that had plagued him for so long. In me, he had cause for hope. After finishing our meals, his ordeal took center stage.

"Tony, I got some of your background from our conversations awhile back, and Leon just gave me an overview before you got here, but what's driving you to help him like you are? I mean what really happened to you?" He reached for a sip from his coffee mug, then focused all his energy on my friend, seriously intent on making some sage contribution to his suffering as well.

Tony was always anxious to tell his story. In our many chats, I felt that I was a far better therapist than any licensed therapist could be. He pulled out his usual flyers from a manila folder and slid them across the table. Then he took us through his odyssey at the Nassau County Courthouse on Long Island where his protracted divorce was literally and physically taking his life from him.

"Well reverend, I had lawyers dragging out my case because there were assets to plunder. If I had only modest means, my divorce would've been done in a matter of months over a decade ago. But there are three judges I've been focused on, spreading the word about their misconduct so they can be removed or at least exposed such that other parents are not victimized by them."

"My gosh, between the two of you guys, you probably had more than fifty judges on your cases."

"Not that many, but close," Tony corrected. He was always anal about facts. "I know Leon's had thirty at least over the same period upstate. I call my lynching the *Trifecta of Judicial Bullies.*"

Even now, I chuckle over that trifecta thing that Tony came up with. As much as he was flat in character, I've heard his lectures enough to know that he can become very entertaining when relating his ordeal. Sometimes you have to spice things up with humor just to stay sane.

We even published a video on You-Tube entitled *Endless Divorce of Professor Anthony Pappas* which still gets me breaking out with laughter. Unfortunately, his story, like mine, is very real and more common than publicly acknowledged across the states.

"Sounds more like horse trading at Belmont than it does a court proceeding," the reverend interjected curiously.

"I wish it was a horse race," Tony reacted, "but here the horse trading was behind closed doors. It starts with Judge Gartenstein. He wasn't even an elected judge but an appointed hearing officer. I made the innocent mistake of sending him an ex-parte letter of complaint."

"Next thing I know, reverend, he's got me in court threatening me with contempt and directing me to keep my hands on the hearing table where he could see them, as if I'm some kind of violent criminal. I was simply reaching inside my suit jacket for eyeglasses."

"Sounds like a scene from Goodfellas, a bit over the top wouldn't you say, Leon."

"That's only the beginning. Keep listening," I urged.

"Gartenstein just couldn't contain his ego," Tony continued. "But when cooler heads prevailed, he offered to get off my case. Whether it was his conscience or more likely a fear of another ethics complaint, I quickly accepted his offer in writing through my attorney. But something I was doing outside the court must have drawn his ire, because he reneged days later and even tried to justify his conduct by referring me to a judicial threats unit. Nothing ever came of that."

"Wow, can he do that Leon? We're talking about Tony here, a distinguished professor at a world class university. Was there anything to support this referral?"

"As I said, just keep listening reverend. Many of these appointed quacks have little conscience and a lot of ego. They can be so shameless with all that unchecked power. You're getting a better drift now behind Tony's obsession with judicial immunity. But that's how judges swat out their gadflies, abusing a highly regarded office and duping the public with their titles of nobility."

Taking the cue, Tony pulled out a copy of an infuriating decision which he routinely kept with him. He shoved it across the table. The page and shaded text were all too familiar to me.

"Look there, reverend, read that. Gartenstein issued a decision comparing me to a terrorist. He writes that my complaints read with 'the idiom used by the perpetrator of the Fort Hood massacre.' That's where Nidal Hasan, an army major and psychiatrist, killed thirteen people and injured another thirty in a mass shooting. Now how can my colorful depictions of corruption be compared to some terrorist manifesto?"

Tony was known for his flowery narratives, but judges do this all the time in their wordy opinions. As for demeanor, he was always deadpan. You could report breaking news that an asteroid was bearing down on his home in Queens, and Tony would simply demur. His crusade was far more earth-shattering. Here just the thought of Gartenstein was producing tremors.

"It's been years since this rag sheet was made a part of the court records, never corrected. I still can't believe I'm reading it. I don't care what I gotta do, but they're not getting away with this."

Reverend Forbes then put on his own glasses. He shook his head upon verifying the depiction.

"Gartenstein also justified his attack by writing for the first time that I caused over $8,000 in reconstructive surgery to my wife's face during a violent marriage. It was all made up. There was no proof of mandatory reporting or medical bills. I mean that would be a Class B felony if true."

"I got nowhere with appeals, publications or commissions," Tony continued. "So I decided to get creative. I went to the district attorney on Long Island and the U.S. Attorney's Office in Brooklyn to report myself as a violent felon and terrorist based on Gartenstein's official findings. If I was so dangerous to get reported to a judicial threats unit, I would have to be investigated, prosecuted and sent to prison. Hell, Leon did nothing like this and look what he's been facing."

"You're kidding," reacted the civil rights advocate with some amusement. "You're actually trying to get arrested by authorities on your own criminal complaint. Am I hearing this right?"

"Yes, to make a point. As I say, there's no judicial accountability and this guy is a public servant. I was hoping to draw attention to what's really going on in these courts. Anyway, there were no arrests, no logic or victim complaint of any kind. So that's when Gartenstein steps down only to be replaced by Judge Falanga. Barely into the case, all upset about the record and my public activity, he issues a gag order so broad that it makes a mockery of our First Amendment."

Tony reached back into his file for another court transcript and read it aloud at the table while other patrons were becoming attracted to our exchanges:

I am admonishing you right now (Professor), you are not to communicate with anybody inside the court system, outside the court system, about how you feel you were being treated or anything like that. If you feel I am violating your right to free speech, you have the absolute right to feel that way and do whatever you feel is appropriate. If I decide to hold you in contempt, we'll cross that bridge when we come to it. Do you understand?

Shifting this time from advocate to citizen, Jim Forbes reacted. "Wow, that is broad. I gotta ask again, Leon, does he have the right to do that? I mean, can a judge stop a university professor outside the court system from expressing his opinions about our judicial branch of government?"

"Hey, you'll have to ask our Supreme Court. I asked the same sort of question there in five separate writs over a ten-year period and they turned me down every time. At least Tony's judge was up front with his order. Mine were usually careful enough to avoid the record. I would rather they simply be honest about it. That way we know where we stand. I called the trickery in my case, contempt by ambush. And you wonder why I'm flying to Paris, far from their reach."

"So where's the third judge in this trifecta?"

"That's Judge Zimmerman. She replaced Falanga. I thought she might relent after I filed a federal lawsuit. But she just adopted what the other judges said and issued a twenty-year protection order against me like I was some kind of sexual predator. There was not even a request for this from my ex, nothing but hallucinations to base it on. Something fired her up."

"Twenty years? I've heard of convicted criminals who get six months on a burglary rap, but two decades? Who were the lawyers involved?"

"Well I was forced to go through many, but my ex-wife had only one at the time due to the benefit of a court order forcing me to pay lawyer fees on both sides of our divorce. I was the 'monied spouse' as they called it even though she was gainfully employed in a school district. Now where's the accountability there?"

"I mean think about it," Tony decried. "She can just spend hours gossiping with her lawyer because I was the one being billed. So ignorant, she was even chipping away at the estate I left for our children in my will. It's like a person with a big lottery win shopping on Fifth Avenue."

"So let me see if I understand this correctly. You're paying your ex's lawyer to keep the litigation going. And he's billing away with no concern for his client's adult children. Then they all show their appreciation by treating you like the worst of criminals. You've never even been arrested!"

Before Reverend Forbes could move to another sermon, I wound up our luncheon because Tony was my ride to JFK. I needed to be overseas before an arrest might become reality in my case. Tony had been trying to get the Archdiocese, Catholic Church, Protestant ministers and Jewish rabbis to join in a declaration against this court system. I was skeptical of his success, but there were players in Manhattan that only he knew. So I made my pitch for what it was worth.

"Reverend, as I see it, religion on all fronts is being conquered by an evil blitzkrieg. It's like the last world war with the allies. People know it's coming, but not a single religion is doing anything about it. We have these huge cathedrals, temples and churches as a testament to our collective belief in a higher power."

"But they're like that Maginot Line," I continued, "a giant disconnected, antiquated fortification that failed to prevent the modern invasion. We can make a pilgrimage to Mecca or Jerusalem but everything from Hollywood to Wall Street is advancing through the Ardennes."

Tony was well schooled in history and the reverend was around to read about the Nazi blitzkrieg when it actually happened. They got my meaning and accepted my own challenge to get our religions united against an evil that was extinguishing them all. So off we went in separate directions to war with Legion and his band of demons loosened from the fires of hell.

Tony's trifecta continued to make its rounds in New York City as my human rights reports soon did in Paris. I concluded our exchange with a proposal for a comprehensive effort at the Justice Department. I had made the case there that this custody epidemic had lingered for decades and was now at levels fatal to the very health, productivity and military defense of our nation.

Sound investigations would have to be commissioned to reverse state sponsored litigant abuse which the federal government had ironically promoted through a funding law. But I left the two with an ominous question after exiting the diner: how do you get diverse victims, all immersed in custody and support wars against one another, to engage in a joint mission of reform?

Unethical Ethics Committee

I knew my mission in Paris would invite graver consequences. After twenty-three unblemished years in the legal profession, I was made subject to a witch hunt by ethics lawyers relying on a loose collection of grievances. But that was their pretext. In reality, they were targeting my whistleblowing activity, the court corruption I was exposing. That "hunt" was so inept it made Dick Cheney out to be an expert marksman. I reported regular misconduct not only among colleagues but these ethics lawyers as well. Their superiors never flinched to give it credence.

A maliciously protracted investigation designed to discredit my reform message drove me to career suicide. Here, you will learn of alarming whistleblower activity that was suppressed across the board. During hearings before the Moreland Commission at Pace University, for example, I accurately described my attackers as an unethical ethics committee, backing that up with the recent termination of its chief counsel and deputy lawyers for falsifying time sheets.

That's right, your eyes are not playing tricks, the standard-bearers of lawyer ethics discharged by their own ethics committee. If you wonder how lawyer bills get so outrageous, these are the watchdogs charged with overseeing unscrupulous billing practices. Their neglect of unethical and orchestrated conflict has harmed more families than adultery, nagging and domestic violence combined. Like Bernie Madoff, they were the foxes watching the chicken coop.

Worse yet, no public charges, ethical or criminal, were ever prosecuted against them. Instead, they were allowed to resign quietly so that harmful publicity could be quelled. [26] Had it been anyone else stealing from a court employer, a prison term would be guaranteed. Ex-governor Rod Blagojevich was sentenced to fourteen years for trying to sell a Senate appointment. On his non-violent crime, it was justified as an example to be made. Where was the example here?

You really have to ponder this a bit. In one of my cases, a city worker was fired for exposing executive raises. He charged $16 on a city gas card for valid reimbursement hours later, then quickly charged with a felony and arrested after a single weekend. I won his verdict in criminal

---

[26] Robert Gavin, *Oversight lawyers quit amid inquiry*, (Albany) Times Union, July 10, 2013

court and then sued the mayor and accomplices in civil court to earn a substantial recovery. [27]

At the Moreland hearings, I compared that case to Bernie Madoff's $70 billion crime spree before he was finally arrested. That outcome took more than a decade. The Commission never responded to my stark analogy. Adding insult to injury, while those ethics lawyers were allowed to resign, I sustained far worse retributions for exposing them on other misconduct.

Maybe your own community, friend or family member was impacted by all this and you never even knew it. To be sure, lawyers on the bench may harbor far greater evil than the ones in their courtroom. Take, for example, my pedophile custody judge, Bryan Hedges, permanently barred from the bench after admitting to sexual abuse of his own handicapped, five-year old, niece. [28] You have to ponder that one as well. I was able to keep my young daughters out of a session in this judge's chambers where parents were not allowed in, known as a Lincoln hearing.

It raises important questions: What sort of perverse thought was the learned Judge Hedges concealing when he interacted with countless little girls? How many were victimized by his untold fantasies? What other sorts of evil lurked in the minds of jurists that should be disclosed? Forget the answers. In one of my highly read postings, I turned the tables by proposing that, like the litigants they monitor, judges should be screened through mandatory psychiatric evaluations.

My proposal was anything but extreme given the forensic preconditions for law enforcement and others with crucial duties, i.e.

---

[27] Rocco LaDuca, *Tanoury Jr. lawsuit settled for $75,000,* (Utica) Observer Dispatch, December 4, 2007

[28] In re Bryan Hedges, 20 NY3d 677 (2013)(Syracuse family court judge permanently removed after resignation)

Nidal Hasan. A long list here can hardly be disputed. The custody judge replacing Hedges in my case, Michael Hanuszczak, was also forced to resign for sexually harassing his court clerks. [29] A city judge, Gerald Popeo, no longer on the bench, was assigned to my custody case years later despite a public censure by a judicial commission for racist remarks and threats from the bench. [30] More on him later. And this is only a sampling from one case.

It is a logical response to judicial immunity which bases itself on a misplaced trust in self-restraint. What self-restraint is trustworthy anymore when Michigan Judge Wade McCree abused the privacy of court chambers to impregnate a litigant, the mother in a child support case? Her adversary was placed on a monitoring device. Judicial immunity was then exploited to deny him recovery in a federal civil rights case. Is adultery in chambers now a protected judicial act? [31]

I did not let such sordid details die in my crusade, and the hornets' nest was now bursting. Every aspect of my life was therefore being scrutinized when I flew to Charles de Gaulle airport. In New York, I was adding to my ordeal with Tony's plethora of corruption which I hoped could attract publicity in my absence. Paris was a city renowned for its dedication to human rights. I would visit every relevant office during my indeterminate stay there to make an impact.

During my long flight across the Atlantic, I recalled an event in 2010 at our nation's capital. I was to be a main speaker at a reform conference with former Georgia Senator Nancy Schaefer. Like me, Nancy had been exposing vast injustices and had just published a book,

---

[29] Debra Cassens Weiss, *Judge resigns after accusations of unwanted kissing*, abajournal. com. September 23, 2020

[30] Staff reporter, *Utica city court judge censured*, uticaod.com, February 23, 2015

[31] Associated Press, *U.S. Supreme Court: No lawsuit against ex-judge McCree*, Detroit News, January 26, 2015

The Corrupt Business of Child Protective Services. She never made it to the podium due to a suspicious murder-suicide involving her husband of fifty-two years. [32] Did I mention I was writing a book?

So that pretty much summed up my predicament on a small hill in the north of Paris. Just another day in Europe. With all that I had endured over the years, I asked myself again whether I made the right decision to be here. But that question had already been answered by court sanctioned alienation of my girls and the countless victims left behind in my homeland. It is why I risked my career, relations and life itself over a David-Goliath battle begging for an underdog victory.

---

[32] Classifiedleaks.com, The Controversial Life and Suspicious Death of Nancy Schaefer, December 7, 2015

CHAPTER 4

THE MAKING OF A WHISTLEBLOWER

Up 'n at 'em. That was my first thought when the sun made its mark on my eyelids at the dawn of my new life. At first, I could not figure out where I was. Then it hit me. I really was here in a room where I could barely squeeze around my bed to the bathroom. The view from my lone window could not pierce the obstacles of a cement kingdom. This was no dream, it was very lucid, a nightmare come true in a foreign land where I could not even speak the language.

I did well in my high school French class, but Mr. Intorcia would not be here for vital assistance. I could still hear him condemning our American way of life while bestowing every accolade on the traditions of the French people. It was not unusual for him to cite examples of disrespect among students running late in the hallway by his classroom door. It's as if he was commissioned by the French president himself. Things that were so fleeting then were so all-important now.

I decided to turn over under my covers away from the menacing light. I would have to remember to push back the shades into that window to block it more effectively before the next morning. Not used to the noise at a nearby elevator, I'm not sure it would do me good anyway. I struggled in vain to re-enter the dream where I left off. My girls were happy at their playground, and I was pushing them alternately on the swings in the yard of my home, a home I might never see again.

They were much older now, and I wondered where they might be at this moment. My musing was followed by an avalanche of worries. Did they need my advice, were they in any trouble, were they driving yet, and the biggest one, did they have boyfriends? A permissive dad, I always assured each that she could date anyone because the three of us would have a great time together. It was never funny to either, but it put a smile on my face, returning me to happier times.

Who knows how much storage is never downloaded from the human brain? But by slowing the "gigabytes" which barrage our bodies each day, I have come to believe it enables long forgotten events to make their way vividly to the forefront. I have often wondered how many others might never be treated to an opportunity like the one I was now enjoying. Whatever the explanation, our minds are a fascinating place to re-live precious times and escape dismal realities.

That blessing would become so valuable when an aging body prevented me from doing the things I took for granted in my youth. I aggressively planned for that day, not in the monetary sense but the physical side. I worked out strenuously and regularly, never an illness since high school. Search in vain and the most you would find are skin conditions and an insurance related check-up during my twenties which raised the false specter of a malignant tumor in my lung.

Unfortunately, with the combined stress today over so many years, I wondered how much longer my body could hold up. Right now, it was full of energy, my legs anxious to send the rest of me off to do whatever it is that it did. But I fought them off. There was simply nowhere to go to satisfy such urges. Days filled with office duties, childrearing and court appointments were now replaced by decadence. No one cared if I was dead or alive, certainly no one in this city.

That painful realization caused me to strike a compromise, an awake adventure of the mind. I simply buried my head in the pillow and reminisced about a wild ride through life so far. I did much more than physical regimen in preparation for old age. I also filled my days with diverse activity, trips to exotic places, and challenges that most shied away from. I was therefore rewarded with a treasure trove of memories to revisit at any moment. It's what kept me sane.

I recalled my senior quote from the yearbook at New York Mills High School. I didn't know much about its origins other than Sir Walter Scott was the author. I loved every word when I came upon it. A mere one-liner but for me spot-on, concisely defining the person I was and the kind of life I wanted to pursue. To this day, I could repeat it at an instant and did so every time I looked upon Walt's statue in Central Park. Here is what he advised me when I was seventeen:

> *One hour of life, crowded to the full with glorious action and filled with noble risks, is worth whole years of those mean observances of paltry decorum.*

My classmates never said much about that quote, probably figuring it suited the guy they knew. It was simply, Leon, whatever the hell he was talking about, the only Regents scholarship winner not selected to the National Honor Society who celebrated the decision with a beer on school grounds. He was the guy who challenged football teammate, Mike Geddes, for the most truant classes in physics only to become two of those passing the Regents exam at the end of the year.

We were proud members of the dreaded "skid row" as our teacher, Henry McCann, called it. Reserved to the two that would never make anything of themselves, it was located at the back of the room. To make his point, he went out of his way to assure that no other student occupied it Such a disgrace never bothered either of us in the least because that row was nearest the door where we could sneak in late while Mr. McCann was preoccupied at the chalk board.

It was a row we could not access on the day our grades were reported because it was filled with classmates as a sign of awe or humor. It was the same day that the chair of the honors committee tried to apologize privately in the hallway. I cut her off with the curt reply that I thought they had made the right decision as there was "no honor to elitism." I never learned what she was thinking as I walked off and didn't care. It was a familiar scene in college, law school and the present day.

Grade School Greeting Cards to Soldiers in Vietnam

As long as I could remember, my mind saw a light that would send me to uncharted territory time and again, to war against serious injustices, including the wars I could not grasp. In Anna Sullivan's third grade class at Kernan School, we were made part of a writing contest to inspire soldiers in Vietnam during the Christmas holidays. Looking back, I must say it was an ingenious overture. But what did I know? I was just doing what I was told, or so she thought.

At the time, there was great political upheaval regarding a war that took over 58,000 American lives. Men in the jungles of Asia were in desperate need of justification for their service to our nation. Creative greeting cards from little boys and girls would be a priceless gift from home, much preferred over the Hallmark variety. Still, it was a risky experiment monitored well beyond our classroom windows and the brainchild of a teacher whose brother was out in those jungles.

Unlike prior wars, children of this one were the first to see vivid depictions of the carnage on nightly television broadcasts. We were exposed to horrors on the other side of the globe which might be considered child abuse by today's child protection agencies. But those images provided fertile ground for creativity through naivety, innocence in place of bombs dropped into the killing fields, a genuine message of love and concern in place of propaganda and conflict.

We were given the choice of writing a composition or a poem for their entertainment. That's it, two choices, and we had to pick one. So off we went, vigorously writing away, cursive in place of cursor, to complete an assignment beyond the capabilities of our tender minds to appreciate. I sensed something out of the ordinary here, so I decided to rise to the occasion. I violated the rules, thereby enabling me to compose something which was evidently quite extraordinary.

Yes, we were given a choice, but it bore no logic as far as I was concerned. I loved to write, and I loved to craft poems. At the time, my gang friends poked fun at sissy poetry. Today, Rap music has turned out countless millionaires. So why should I be censored? Besides, no one said that a child could not write a composition with a poem inside of it, a home run for war heroes as far as I was concerned. So that's what I did, indifferent to the disciplinary consequences.

It's been suggested that I should reproduce that composition here in its entirety, but I'm not falling for that. I've been humiliated enough over the years. Assuredly there were parts about guns hurting ears and bombs bursting in the air. And tanks. I loved tanks, so that was in there too. It had to pick up a smile for some. Others might treat it as incidental plagiarism of Francis Scott Keyes, but these colorful images were better traced to the sixties' television series, *Combat*.

At the time, my dad would take me to ride the tanks at the Sylvan Beach Amusement Park. They're still there by the way, looking the same as they did way back then. My daughters can verify from the days they rode them as well. Those tanks did wonders to cheer me up whenever I was ill, and in my early years that was often. I had contracted just about everything a poor neighborhood could offer, landing in the hospital with a near death condition more than once.

To my relief, I did not get a detention. Instead, I won the prize. Before you knew it, media crews were showing up at our humble home on Saratoga Street in west Utica. A single alley on one side to access a tiny back yard and a kitchen that could barely fit a handful of people. It was anything but "white privilege" and where my very first unsolicited news conference was conducted. Very shy, I never saw my mom and dad beaming with pride as they were that day. So I just did it.

In those days, kids had to wear black ties and suits for such occasions. My picture ended up on the front page of the Utica (New York) Observer Dispatch. That's when the city's population exceeded 100,000. More humiliating, my entire poem was reproduced beneath it for my gang friends to ridicule on the streets. But the rewarding aspect of this exhibition was that my greeting card was the one selected to go to my teacher's brother.

Unearned College Degrees

Decades later I was elected to the city council. It turned out that a retired school teacher named Anna Sullivan became one of my constituents and an avid supporter. Fortunately, my little sister retained a copy of that old news article so that the story you just read could not be exploited for "dishonesty" by my ethics monitors. Hard as that may be to believe, they would likely become the first to scrutinize this book. Rule 8.4(c) of the ethics rules provides that a lawyer shall not "engage in conduct involving dishonesty, fraud, deceit or misrepresentation."

Are you kidding me? Practicing lawyers and those on the bench are doing that every day in every courthouse across America. Juries struggle constantly to decide which of two or more competing sides is telling the truth and they sometimes convict the innocent. Who among us cannot be violated for "dishonesty?" It's the one rule my adversaries exploited the most to censor me. If you think I'm being oversensitive regarding that long ago article, the witch hunt against me started in 2008 with that collection of grievances covering a period into the prior decade.

Among the inquiries I was required to answer, there was a gossip site the same year which contained an anonymous post regarding my fictitious lawsuit against Dunkin Donuts. It was obviously made up to humor the one against McDonalds resulting in that outrageous hot coffee verdict. Since there was no formal grievance, that made this inquiry a double anonymous, one on the non-issue of practicing law with a suspended license four years later. It gets better.

Family court jurists gave me a PhD and Master's degree I never earned in a May 3, 2013 and July 29, 2013 decision. They did this to concoct a higher child support order perhaps with the delusional belief I would not discover them. Concededly such decisions were so routinely negative that a detailed review became a gesture in futility. I was obviously being set up for contempt incarceration. Even after I corrected them, they refused to remove those degrees from the record or consideration in the support formula, making them the *law of the case.*

Simply stated, these judges, James Gorman and Daniel King, conferred upon me degrees that no university could. Now if that's not "dishonesty, fraud, deceit or misrepresentation," then I don't know what is. The federal court, state appeals courts and judicial conduct commission never mentioned these phantom degrees or this unprecedented *law of the case.* Not one judge did a thing to correct it. Doesn't that make them all co-conspirators in a fraud upon the public?

I mean if you make an honest mistake, I can let that slide. But this was not "harmless error" as the latter judge tried to rationalize before giving me his degree. If a gross factual error is clearly raised and you still refuse to correct it out of pure ego or hatred, then the dishonesty becomes willful, systemic and the worst kind of misrepresentation because it comes from a judge. These are public servants held in the highest regard. Here they were coming unglued in their revenge.

With no commencement ceremony, I therefore decided to accept the unearned degrees. This had the benefit of allowing me use of the title, doctor, in my continued reform efforts. And that only infuriated them all the more since the public generally retains far greater respect for doctors than lawyers. It does not mean I have agreed to be as deceitful. I did earn a Juris Doctor degree as a condition for becoming a lawyer, but we rarely employ the doctor title except as professors.

This sort of fearless protest earned me the label, *Honey Badger,* and a target status like no lawyer I have ever known. Indeed, after another anonymous grievance influenced by a now deceased lawyer dated January 18, 2017, my condition got so tenuous that I offered a manuscript of my pending book to New York's high court for approval. I never did get a response, but a licensing court again denied me reinstatement on April 13, 2017 and yet again on September 17, 2020.

There were too many years of censorship by that Third Department court which I compared to the Third Reich. True story. That may seem extreme, but in contrast with other courts, this one failed to present my side of arguments in any reinstatement decision. If it's not mentioned, it didn't happen, yet another insulation tactic. I was simply responding with the same boldness as the retaliation I was receiving. It compelled me to clear my publications with the high command.

So if you're still here reading this, you're in good company. My work has been monitored by judges, politicians, investigators, lawyers, maybe even an Indian chief. It even attracted Donald Trump's lawyer in 2016. As stated, in the same year, my exposures incurred a family court gag order on my website, removed after I challenged it in New York Supreme

Court. Seven of its postings were recklessly attached to a confidential ethics report dated April 8, 2014. One was merely a dedication to my deceased mother. Never was I charged or sued regarding them.

The college degrees I actually did earn came no easier than my valid public criticisms. In third grade, I already knew what I wanted to be when I grew up. I needed no guidance counselor, and fortunately so, because the one at my high school was useless. I was pretty much self-taught through avid reading and a connection with the real world. Indeed, I had no mentor for my earliest court arguments and jury trials, yet I put together a perfect record of acquittals.

In a normal professional life, I would have no need to cite my accomplishments. But in this one, I was forced to do it to defend myself like my dad did while employed in a steel mill. The union protected him there like the brothers of a war platoon. These heroes on the domestic front were also protecting my little brother, two sisters and the rest of my family with a stay-at-home mom. Here, of course, there was no such protection, so I had to construct my own unique fortification.

Unfortunately, the reality was that my dad could not afford to send me to Cornell or Columbia where I wanted to go. Even though a recruiter from a prestigious school solicited me in our living room, the bottom line was a closed door. My grades tanked after that. And this might shed some light for the goody two-shoes who felt my skid row reply to our honors committee was so disrespectful. The road to success in my world was blocked by countless trials and tribulations.

The lesson I learned then is that merit often did not matter in the scheme of things. When you remove fair treatment, you destroy much more than merit, you crush dreams. The best do not rise to the top, and society is worse off for it. It was a lesson which proved to become a great motivation in the civil rights litigation I won later on. Whenever some self-loving politician or elitist law firm was my adversary, I worked extra hard to humiliate him or her at every turn.

Audacity in Auditing Class

In any event, resigned to my temporary fate as an accountant, those grades bottomed out at Mohawk Valley Community College which I treated as a lay-over to my true destination. I also got a chance to live life, the kind of experiences that so many upper level types could only dream of having. Next stop, the State University of New York where I made a resounding academic come-back. Still, fate, or more aptly a miracle was necessary for my road to the New York bar.

I was enrolled in an auditing class which had me craving for an alternate career as the custodian who entered our room briefly each morning. We had to complete audit reports for review by the professor at each stage of development. I didn't mind the numbers challenge, I had excelled in math, algebra and calculous in high school, but there were entire pages of fictitious events which we were required to reproduce verbatim from our textbooks to make the report look official.

For me, it was just another example of elitism masked by rampant plagiarism. If nothing else it was a complete waste of time better spent at the college pub while the drinking age was still eighteen. When it came time to submit our complete audit reports at the end of the semester, I came up with a ruse which I thought was sure-fire. A better thought would have been backfire.

I would open and close each reproduced text exactly as it appeared in our textbooks. Confident that my professor would skip over the parts common to all reports, I inserted deviant phrases in the body of my text. None of it was vulgar but definitely hysterical if gauged by the number of confidants falling off their bar stools at the pub when I shared it with them. I added the analytical components as our genuine work product and the only parts relevant to the merits.

I was out to make a point, a sort of academic protest, but it backfired terribly when the professor began summarizing his review and grades on the last day of classes. Mine was singled out and made the example for those who would dare to question authority. Not only was I given my first failing grade, but I was being referred to the academic vice-president for further action.

Desperate to save my career as an accountant, I was able to get a meeting with him. I explained how I meant no disrespect but a sort of class critique to improve the curriculum. He laughed harder than my confidants did at the pub.

Now here was a challenge fit for a lawyer focused on nothing less than all hope of passing the character and fitness requirements for admission to the bar. I resorted to an ultimate defense, one I would later learn to be mitigation. After stressing my life impacts, the professor relented with a re-assignment requiring every word to be reproduced.

Life was not easy as a principled gladiator, and this was one of many early challenges that I had long buried in the darkest recesses of my mind. It was unearthed years later at a coffee table in our local Sangertown Square Mall. A financial analyst had joined me with a group of political types reminiscing about our college days. He contributed that last day in class, how everyone was aghast at my "audacity in auditing class" as he put it. I came away from that reminder with a distinct impression that one of my confidants was a competitive snitch. So much for a fair test.

Campus or No Campus

At the same college, my survival skills may have led to the survival of the very campus where this professor made his living. I was elected student body president. For me it was little more than a campaign to upset Mr. Popularity. I won by only nine votes. Nine people changed my life forever. But by the time my administration ended, we had launched our first intercollegiate sports program, the name "wildcats" was adopted, and the following story became a part of its history.

That election entitled me to become the only student member of the administrative council. The college president and his elite group of doctorates were happy to have me on-board in place of my predecessor who boycotted the bulk of those meetings in protest over something I cannot recall. He was a biker, a returning student much older than the rest of us, and a throw-back from the volatile sixties. He was also my fraternity president anxious to influence me out of the gate.

Our campus had been holed up in temporary facilities at a crumbling textile mill long past its scheduled transition to a new campus to be built on an 800 acre site in Marcy, New York. Like a lot of things in New York, this massive capital project got caught up in politics, leaving students innocent victims to an endless harangue over campus sites. That debate had been settled by the purchase of agricultural land just outside the city. But as I learned, in politics, nothing is certain.

New York's Lieutenant Governor at the time was Mario Cuomo, father of the later governor, Andrew Cuomo. Along with Utica's Mayor Stephen Pawlinga, then Governor Hugh Carey and some local power brokers anxious to unload cheap land near the railroad tracks, a downtown campus was born. Opposing it on the Republican side was a collection of minority members of the state Assembly led by a powerhouse member of the Senate named James Donovan.

Jim was also chair of the Senate Education Committee. Among those in his war camp was a not-so-neutral college president named William Kunsela. Ethics prevented him from weighing in on this growing debate, and he was expressly prohibited by the university chancellor. But there was no rule against collaborating with a member of his administrative council, the only one outside of any chain of command. Fatefully, that person was me, again called upon to rise to an occasion.

Time was of the essence because the Marcy site was facing a political blitzkrieg. Impressive renditions had already been drawn up by elite architects to compare a new downtown site with those in neighboring Syracuse and Buffalo. It was a poor comparison which I could verify from my adventures there as a child. But to the warring factions, the students became a prize target for influencing this debate. I was summoned to City Hall along with fellow student leaders.

Then Mayor Stephen Pawlinga was an accomplished trial attorney. Hence it was no shock that he would give us a powerful closing statement regarding his downtown campus. He also assured us that he had the support of the big players in Albany. Therefore it would behoove us to get on the winning side right away. We were being treated like dignitaries until I countered his elaborate presentation with two city campus options which earned me a "stay-away" order at City Hall.

I offered a proposal at the former state hospital grounds in west Utica already owned by the state and another being promoted by a local political activist named David Ashe. Both made all the sense in the world and the latter was ideally located among stately homes once occupied by famous Uticans along Park Avenue and Rutger Street. Greek Row was already constructed. My classmates thought I went bonkers, and suddenly I was ostracized by both major camps.

However, my approach was a subterfuge. I was not out to support any downtown campus but to expose its corrupt underpinnings. If the mayor could not explain how his site by the noisy tracks was superior to the more logical alternatives, the whole idea would collapse since there was no big money to be pocketed. I had already hosted news conferences at our student offices but was rudely shaken from my naivety when discovering how the media could misreport them.

SUNY College of Technology was now mired in a very serious stalemate. As the site proposals grew to include co-location with the private Utica College, then a part of Syracuse University, powerful figures in Albany were calling for a closure of the old mill campus with a partitioning of its fledgling departments for annexation by competing state campuses. It reminded me of the partitioning of Poland by Russia, Germany and Austria during our Revolutionary period.

Regionally, we were among the weakest politically with Syracuse only fifty miles to the west, Albany ninety miles to the east and Binghamton with an established university center to the south. Indeed after our former student president spoke at a public hearing before the statewide university Board of Trustees, its chairman concluded that we might never get a campus as long as he was enrolled there. I followed with one that drew a standing ovation from campus delegates throughout the state. Even the chairman rose to shake my hand.

Faced with shaky prospects, I prevailed upon student leaders to endorse candidates for mayor and county executive who publicly supported a Marcy campus. Louis LaPolla was one of them, but he lost to Steve Pawlinga the same year. The other, Sherwood Boehlert, won by a narrow margin eventually succeeding to Congress. I was then made subject to a protest by student dissidents condemning my foray into politics, so I had to come up with something extraordinary.

$9 Million Picnic

Embattled and desperate for survival, I came up with an idea so out-of-the-box that it turned the tide of campus debate once and for all.

I called it the Nine Million Dollar Picnic. Fed up with the abuse and politics, I exploited the financial commitment already made by the state to a site otherwise valued at only a few hundred dollars per acre. College administrators assured me that it was a figure exceeding $9 million, a lot of money in those days.

The students would have a $9 million picnic at taxpayer expense on the campus site since there was nothing else being done with vacant land for the students it was intended to benefit. We had no viral internet back then, but news of our creative picnic protest spread with the speed of an express train on the downtown railroad tracks. We even got a call from CBS 60 Minutes, a news organization which featured me in an interview twenty years later.

It was all going too well until I was summoned to a meeting by President Kunsela to discuss our picnic with his college administrators. I was expecting compliments but was threatened with arrest instead. Bill Kunsela was a no-nonsense dictator who reminded me of my high school coach, Ben Ross, a former marine. When he barked out an order, the entire college shook. Even my auditing professor might hide behind his desk. But this would not yield the same outcome. I was not going to plead. A nobody at age twenty-one, I was not going to back down to anyone.

My picnic caper had seriously inflamed both warring factions on this campus debate. Evidently it had everyone looking bad. Now how was I supposed to anticipate that? By not getting formal permission to spend a few hours on our own campus site, one that our tuition was supposed to permit, I would be arrested for trespass. As the leader of this coup, I would be made the example once again for an act which defied authority.

Unlike auditing class, this was a stand-off far more impacting on any future character and fitness review by the New York bar. Throwing caution to the wind, I informed the college president and his submissive elite that the picnic was going forward, they were all invited, and I will be there for my first ever arrest. I then got up from the conference table and politely exited Mill Building Number Two. As the only one being threatened, this time I shared my rebellion with no one.

Fortunately, there was a player in this mix who loved my idea. He happened to be president of the college alumni association and son of the Senator Jim Donovan. Jerry had already prepared a giant banner for this picnic endorsing the Marcy campus site. As for the student population, attendees were growing by the hour. They were even coming up with creative attention-getters such as classrooms in the pasture cordoned off with ropes. There were makeshift professors like my fraternity president offering lectures under the course title, "Principles of Civil Unrest."

This was all getting seriously out of control. These were not my course offerings, but how could I quell such enthusiasm? And if I was going to be jailed for trespass, it was not going to happen quietly into the night. Things took a major turn for the better when the senator himself issued a news release announcing his attendance followed by other dignitaries.

Finally, on the morning of the event, I arrived not to a squad of state troopers but work crews who had already removed the road barriers and supplied various essentials for a picnic. The event was a resounding success, my right to counsel was put off for another day, and news of the vast waste of tax dollars spread exponentially across the state.

Exactly two months later, after a narrow victory as an independent (defeated in the Democrat Primary by Louis LaPolla), Mayor Pawlinga shifted positions and endorsed the site. He joined me, Senator Donovan, Bill Kunsela and fellow students at the college for a victory celebration when the SUNY Board of Trustees announced their renewed commitment to a Marcy campus.

After those harrowing events, I was once again summoned to a meeting with Bill Kunsela. Only this time it was private. He asked me what my plans were after graduation. Not inclined to admit my long held goal, I fell back on the more attainable one of Certified Public Accountant. To my dismay, he was not pleased with that answer at all. He hesitated a bit, sat back in lofty chair and then asked if I had ever thought of pursuing the legal profession.

Suddenly my high school guidance counsellor had made a rebound in the flesh. If Bill thought so highly of my prospects, then I was not so crazy after all. To think it took this long for someone to see my calling, and what better recommendation than one from a New York university president. I then spilled my guts and he quickly responded with a call to his college placement personnel.

I treated the Law School Admission Test like an appetizer, and soon enough I was off to law school. I delivered the commencement address at the Utica Memorial Auditorium that year followed by an astronaut of the Apollo mission, a prelude to a college destined to achieve great things. Ultimately it became an elaborate campus under the title SUNY Polytechnic Institute.

I heaped praises on everyone from Bill Kunsela to our families, college staff and even campus security for teaching me so many lessons with their parking tickets. It drew laughter and another parking ticket on my windshield in the lot shortly after we all dispersed. It was voided with well wishes on its face. At that moment, I was beaming on the would-be downtown campus grounds.

I pretty much disappeared from the scene after graduation. Campus plans went forward, and the first building was dedicated as Kunsela Hall in 1985, a matter of parking spaces away from the site of our $9 million picnic six years earlier. Donovan Hall was next as financial commitments grew to many times that figure. Kunsela auditorium was filled to capacity when the new campus was also showcased. There were faculty, alumni, students and dignitaries from all walks of life.

I had just been conferred my law degree and was hired by a downtown law firm. Bill delivered an inspiring history of our new campus, one that almost never was. He singled out many for recognition, and I was the only former student in that group. He welcomed me as a lawyer to verify the promising aspects of a fledgling institution, an achievement he privately promoted but nearly foreclosed at different times of an amazing ride through my undergraduate studies.

Law School Dean Humiliated

I wish I could tell you that I learned my lesson at that point on this journey through academia, but alas that lawyer achievement almost never happened. Shortly into my studies at Northern Illinois University, College of Law, our new Swen Parson Hall was to be dedicated with then Supreme Court Justice Harry Blackmun as the keynote speaker.

Law school dean, Leonard Strickman, was ecstatic about his auspicious affair. He had been highly recruited as an influential scholar from Boston College and even brought some east coast colleagues with him to the delight of the university president. A campus which dwarfed my undergraduate counterpart, the student population here exceeded 25,000. It was a proud Midwest institution anxious to make its mark in the world with a newly accredited law school.

That made Dean Strickman all but untouchable on this campus despite earning some disdain among tenured locals. He was also earning more than the university president himself. None of this interested me much. I was anxious for something far more important. I had never known a real university campus like this. It was part of the

Mid-American Conference, and they even had a football stadium. I still root for their teams today.

NIU was also a teachers' college from the time of its origin. That meant a wide selection of attractive and intellectual undergraduates to meet. Soon enough I had a wonderful girlfriend who invited me to family affairs in suburban Chicago. That made home in New York feel less remote. And while she was preoccupied with her studies, I teamed up with my law school mate, Dan O'Connor. We were out whenever classes got the best of us, and that was fairly often.

Before long I became a sort of reliable social chairman at the law school dormitory where I shared a room during my first year with a guy who never stayed overnight on weekends. The intensity of competitive studies became too overwhelming for any stay longer than necessary. Along the way, I befriended future judges and prominent litigators of Chicago. It was all good until one day when I learned of a schedule change regarding our meal plan at the law dorm.

To elevate the stature of Strickman's gala, one of the weeks of our first break from classes would be switched with the undergraduate schedule so that the dedication ceremony could occur while the vast part of the student population was gone. That way it would not be so hectic. There may have been other reasons, but it was all elitist to me. It also meant that we were on our own as far as any meal plan because it did not pay to have food services open to a handful of law students.

That wasn't really a big deal, not for me anyway. Prior to accepting admission to law school, I had spent two years as a manufacturing supervisor for a Fortune 500 firm. My goal there was to gain practical experience for my management degree while earning reserve funds for law school. But one day I was listening to a petite law student in one of our dorm rooms. Her plan was to forego meals during that week and survive on the supermarket rations that she could afford.

It was all I needed to hear. I started a petition challenging the Dean's action as a breach of our meal contract. Now you really have to ponder that last sentence for a moment. I was in a first year contracts class with only a handful of lectures under my belt. My adversary was not only a contract expert, but a university dean who largely controlled my destiny. I was literally accusing him of willfully violating a contractual agreement between a law school and its law students.

But as far as I was concerned, this was a no-brainer as my classmates thought I was proving it literally. There was no way that the dedication ceremony could be rescheduled and less chance that university facilities were going to be opened for food service. It was too late for all that, and we were even being made to feel that we were lucky to have our law dorm opened at all. A few brave souls joined me for a meeting with the Dean but our petition was turned down.

That's when I did the unspeakable. I went over his head, appealing his denial up the university ladder. To my pleasant surprise, I was successful to the point where the university president himself overruled Dean Strickman. A voucher plan became the solution. That simply meant that the university would cover our meal expenses in the surrounding community for that week. My fellow tenants were elated, and that should've ended the dispute. However, that was not to be.

The dedication of Swen Parson Hall was a resounding success. We all had our pictures taken with Justice Blackmun, author of the abortion decision in *Roe v Wade*. But shortly afterward, our law school's selections for the National Moot Court Competition were announced by Assistant Dean Lenny Mandel, one of Strickman's transplants from Boston. It was based on performances during our first-year, inner school competition. I was notably absent from the two-team listing.

I had scored highly in the minds of other participants including the local associate dean who presided over one of my arguments. Even my teammate in that first year who was selected stated that I deserved to go to the national competition ahead of him. Like the contract grievance, I was pressed to challenge this, but it would go no further than Dean Strickman, this time as an internal matter of the law school. The excuse given by Mandel is that my grades did not make the cut.

Nonsense! This was an intercollegiate competition in which the best advocates, like the best ball players, would advance our university prestige. I was forced to eat the result but not the injustice. I took it upon myself to prove my dean wrong on principle alone. Looking over my class record, at that point nearing final exam time, it did not look good. I had missed all but two family law classes, and the professor nearly removed me on the test day for lack of familiarity.

But I did get a few breaks with an extension to complete a writing project. I recorded a 3.45 grade point average for the semester I was rejected for the national team. I was then vindicated when Dean Strickman was forced to put me on his Dean's List and I went on to win second place in the state competition sponsored by the Illinois bar. Go figure. It featured family law.

Everything culminated on graduation day, our third year, when Dean Strickman finally made peace. To the dismay of most, I was given an award from the American Bar Association in State, Urban and Local Government Law based on my article and GPA of that semester. My dad flew to Chicago and added a few relatives there to witness the unexpected honor. In the end, that was far more precious than any fictitious court competition. And if you're still wondering, they lost.

CHAPTER 5

JUDGE PARIS CALLS PARIS

So, well said Sir Walter Scott. I lived by your ideals. Maybe you knew me better than anyone else did at the time. But you never mentioned pain and suffering, trial and tribulation in that quote. You would be interested to know, however, that there was something you did mention that was censored by a yearbook advisor, the one offering various quotes from a list of literary giants. That's right, no point in turning over in your grave because I got you covered.

With time made available by my persecutors I researched this Walter Scott fellow and learned some remarkable things applicable to my ordeal today. First, the full uncensored quote:

> *One hour of life, crowded to the full with glorious action and filled with noble risks, is worth whole years of those mean observances of paltry decorum, <u>in which men steal through existence, like sluggish waters through a marsh without either honour or observation</u>.*

Prophetically, the censored portion underscored the rest of my story, the abuse by lawyers and former lawyers on the family court bench who steal the substance of parent-child relationships by their existence. The judges are heralded as "Your Honor" but only by observation in their robes when they rule without genuine oversight. What were my high school censors thinking? Did they mean to insulate their trusting students from the real world they were sending us to?

Here are some other quotes, their full text, from Sir Walter Scott which simply cannot be explained in terms of their sheer fateful relevance to my plight decades later:

> *A lawyer without history or literature is a mechanic, a mere working mason; if he possesses some knowledge of these, he may venture to call himself an architect.*
>
> *Revenge is the sweetest morsel to the mouth that was ever cooked in hell.*
>
> *Oh, poverty parts good company.*
>
> *All men who have turned out anything have had the chief hand in their own education.*
>
> *True love's the gift which God has given to man alone beneath the heaven.*
>
> *O, what a tangled web we weave, when first we practice deceit.*
>
> *For he that does good, having the unlimited power to do evil, deserves praise not only for the good he performs, but the evil he forbears.*

There was another relevant passage from my yearbook, but one sponsored by the graduating class ahead of me. I don't know the author, no one is disclosed from the New York Mills Class of '75, but despite its nostalgic prose, it still resonates nearly a half century later. I was fortunate to be part of a very special high school. Maybe you had a similar inspiration from yours. Today I dare say that such passages no longer exist. For that reason alone, I will reproduce it here:

IMPRESSIONS

Maybe this is the hundredth time that you are leafing through these pages. Can you again capture those feelings- the intensity of the excitement, the anger, the quicksilver, joy and sorrow, the feeling of awe each time you discovered something new and meaningful, the desperate desire to do right now mingled with the reluctance to let your dreams for the future drift away. Will you ever again nurture such powerful ideas that were yours alone, that you tried to communicate to others, but that were usually shared, you found, by someone else, and that too often left you confused and frustrated. For who else but you really knew the nervous excitement of curtain time on opening night, the agony of losing by two points because you missed the basket, the warm glow of a friend's praise, and the bittersweet silence of your last look at a now-empty football field. But you were always bound to think another thought, forever looking up and out ahead.

Now, looking back at the lengthening shadows which are slowly descending upon your increasingly distant youth, you may be willing to admit all that you learned in those years. You might even be wondering when it was that you changed... But, think again, look once more, try to recall- that was you. You've experienced, grown, matured- but have you really changed that much? Aren't you still you- the values you live by, the hopes you harbor, the dreams you've dreamed and will go on dreaming? They will be forever yours, always be a part of you... those years.

Right now, these quotes and memories were paying off handsomely, far better than any riches I could have stowed away in a bank. After all, none of us is guaranteed tomorrow. A best friend in grade school died of leukemia before he could make that yearbook. A girlfriend was killed by a drunk driver in junior high, two schoolmates I knew succumbed to AIDS during a promising run in Manhattan's Theatre District, my cycling partner took his life before the age of thirty-five, and a president of our local bar dropped dead on the courtroom floor not long ago. He was forty-six.

Such memories also brought home all that precious time lost with my daughters as they completed their own years in high school, the fathering time erased because of a "custodial parent" masquerading as a mom, those gurus in robes who could not contain their egos, lawyers fleecing our joint child support who could not restrain their greed, and all the other family court predators playing by rules that were routinely skewed in favor of the system. My girls were deprived so much, and yet they will never know just how much.

These thoughts were too painful, but they gave purpose to each morning that I awoke to my current nightmare. Fortunately, my reminiscing would not last. It was only a matter of time before the maid would come knocking with her translation for housekeeping. So out of my bunker I went and into the streets of sunny Paree, confident that no one would be looking for me here. I was free as a bird. But by the end of my first week, that comfort zone would be shattered.

Touring Paris for Human Rights

I began my days in Paris with a goal of sharing a mandamus petition with human rights agencies and international media outlets. In lay terms, this was an extraordinary lawsuit permitted in upper courts to raise vital constitutional questions (certiorari), enforce ministerial acts (mandamus) or challenge lower court authority (prohibition). Rarely granted, it is reflected by the one I filed in New York Supreme Court in 2016 resulting in the removal of that gag order on my website.

I had filed the federal petition in an appeals court in Manhattan before boarding my plane at JFK. It was brought against that federal judge in our state capital, Gary Sharpe, who had announced a human gene not to be discovered by scientists "for another fifty years." And he used this gene to render a sentencing decision. [33] So bizarre, he was

---

[33] United States v Cossey, 632 F.3d 82 (2nd Cir. 2011)

soundly removed from that case by the same appeals court, but as a life tenured jurist, he was later assigned to my fourth civil rights case.

Given the targeting of me, I took the position that Gary should have resigned or been referred for impeachment on grounds that his genetic theories were Hitleresque. They clearly had no place in an American forum. After all, despite the higher court condemnations of the Sharpe gene, how could any litigant know what lurks in the mind of a quack? Such criticisms were a regular feature on my website tagged to such judges resulting in first page disclosures on any Google search. It's one of many tactics in my underground arsenal used to counter media and Big Tech censorship.

More on Gary later, but for purposes of my crusade in Paris, the petition proved to be an ideal summary of human rights violations that were being suppressed in America's divorce courts. It was autumn here, and the temperatures seemed more comfortable than those back in New York. Armed with my briefcase and a stack of copies, I set out for the offices located by way of an old-fashioned street map. I took few risks with an i-phone or computer that could be tracked.

Having argued cases in Manhattan for over two decades, it was not a problem reverting to the archaic method. This would also be good practice in the event of a catastrophic solar flare. I avoided cab costs by walking as much as a hundred blocks each day that I was playing paper boy. I loved those walks, they were so refreshing. In formal attire, I could not run, and that gave the smog less impact. I rarely set up strict appointments. Usually my visits were spontaneous or at the convenience of my targeted offices. It proved to be quite stress-free.

Typically, I would come off the hill on the opposite side of my hotel below Sacred Heart Basilica to begin my assignments. Never exposing myself to a routine, sometimes I would take Boulevard Barbes directly south, other times zig-zagging along streets or rues as they are called here. I journeyed for both tourist and business purposes, seizing upon an office plaque for a random stop whenever a helpful agency escaped my research. The human rights variety was scattered.

Many of the offices visited were poorly staffed and others accessible only through security passes. Some of the representatives I addressed were visibly taken aback by the identities of my persecutors. They acted as if this sort of thing occurred only in totalitarian states or communist countries, not the United States or free world with which they were generally aligned.

One example was Angela Charlton, Chief of the Bureau at the Associated Press office at 162 rue du Faubourg Sainte-Honore. Ideally located between Place de la Concorde near center city and the Arc de Triomphe on the west side, the building also housed a Starbucks where I could get coffee and organized before presentations. I made several visits to the AP office here, and Ms. Charlton seemed veritably interested in my one-man crusade in her city. However nothing ever came of it even though I kept her in the loop. She thanked me for that on one occasion by e-mail.

At the Arc, I had to get an impressive photo to match its grandeur and purpose. The Arc of Triumph was commissioned by Napoleon in 1806 at the peak of the French Empire. It honors those who fought in the revolutionary and Napoleonic wars. Various military heroes are inscribed on its walls, and the Tomb of the Unknown Soldier of World War I is found here.

My favorite French hero was not Napoleon, Lafayette or even Charlemagne, but the General Marquis de Montcalm. He was a key figure in the last of the French and Indian Wars which planted the seeds for our own Revolution. He is most noted for his victory over the British at Fort William-Henry at the southern end of Lake George, New York, my stomping grounds for many years. James Fenimore Cooper wrote about him in his novel, *Last of the Mohicans*, which also became a blockbuster movie in 1992.

But as far as I was concerned, his victories there and in Canada paled in comparison to the one at Fort Ticonderoga in 1758. Infuriated by Montcalm's massacre at William-Henry the year before, the British amassed 15,000 troops at the same location in one of the greatest war flotillas ever to be assembled on a lake. It was also an imperialist conquest masked by revenge in the largest military force put into any battle to that point in time on the American continents.

They advanced under the command of General James Abercromby but defeated by 3,500 troops under Montcalm on the north end at Fort Ticonderoga (Carillon as it was called then). I traced the route of this flotilla many times with my boat and jet skis and even based my own novel, *Voyage to Armageddon*, on some of these events. With my daughters, I met a descendant of Montcalm at a reception commemorating the 1757 battle at Fort William Henry Hotel in 2007.

It was therefore important to look the part when getting my photo taken at the Arc. I asked a group of Asian tourists to do the honors in reciprocation for the ones I had just taken of them. We could not translate but compensated through internationally recognized semaphores and facial gestures. I tried different poses as traffic sped around us. None of it was working. I had never seen so many forms of negative responses. There was simply a regular shaking of heads.

These were perfectionist photo takers, so I thought of striking a Vladimir Putin pose by offering to take my shirt off. After all, this was a world class city and I was moved by a world leader who put his money where his mouth was, promoting good health by example. I mean, let's face it, in politics, it's do as I say but not as I do. Unfortunately, my Asian friends screamed disapproval. Ultimately, we landed a photo compromise that everyone agreed was sufficiently masculine.

These walks across Paris also gave me a better perspective on my new neighbors. I could get to know the diverse people who made this city their home while taking in the magnificent sites at leisure with each district conquered. A variety of languages could be discerned from one block to the next. It was truly a cosmopolitan city reflective, in part, of the country's imperialist history.

On one occasion, I was working my way through the Tenth Arrondissement along the avenue of the saints as I came to name it. It was a string of boulevards ending at Place de la Republic. They included Boulevards Saint-Dennis and Saint-Martin. I could not help noticing the shapely figures of pedestrians everywhere. Drawn to the feminine variety, I conducted an unofficial survey over a thirty block stretch, counting only three women that I considered overweight.

It may be that the expansive lay-out of Paris had a bit to do with this. In the spirit of Pierre L'Enfant who designed Washington D.C. and Georges-Eugene Haussmann who redeveloped Paris, key destinations were far apart. Parks, squares and boulevards were large and many. I generally had less physical demand in cities like New York or Montreal, basically contained islands. Athens, London, Chicago, San Francisco and so many others appeared more centralized.

When I reached Republic Square, I paused to take in the splendor of this rectangular park bordered by cafes, boutiques and restaurants. Rising high above it all in the center was the Monument de la Republic, or the bronze statue of Marianne, commemorating the establishment of the French Republic. Surrounded by three subordinate statues personifying liberty, equality and fraternity, it highlighted the nation's premier values.

It was also the main theme of the new president's inauguration parade on May 14, 2017. At age thirty-nine, Emmanuel Macron became the youngest post-war president of France. Fraternity is the obvious addition concerning the same ideals of the United States. If we can substitute "justice for all" to mean the same thing, President Macron could easily have welcomed my mission. As I would later learn, there was also a dissatisfaction with custody practices here.

This square was the site of the largest ever rally against Islamic terrorism on January 15, 2015. Well over one million people gathered here along with prominent world leaders after forty people were killed in an attack upon a satirical newspaper office and kosher market. It failed to prevent a greater attack on November 13, 2015 which claimed 130 lives at a stadium and theatre.

How ironic, therefore, that I should be here as a free speech victim of a nation whose own president at the time, Barack Obama, never attended this rally. He was the professed leader of the free world and recipient of the 2009 Nobel Peace Prize under peculiar circumstances. But that would not be my only irony.

I was taking in the scene when suddenly my i-phone rang. Expecting some news back home, I carried it in my suit jacket on this day. It had two distinctive rings, one for my friend John and another for Lora Cohen. The latter had reconnected with me as she typically did during our break-ups with lovers. We had met during our twenties and remained caring friends. This ring was neither, sending stress signals throughout my body regarding my life's destiny.

Complexity Insulates Corruption

The phone number showing up on my screen was an official one. I recognized it from the Syracuse courthouse, ground zero for the record number of trial level jurists assigned to my originally uncontested divorce. It turned out to be Judge Anthony Paris calling me direct from state supreme court chambers. Now how often does that occur in world events, a judge named Paris in the United States calling a litigant in Paris, France for a case conference?

Tony Paris was a long tenured judge and well regarded not only among colleagues and lawyers but plain folks everywhere. A great sense of humor, he was adept at settling cases for the good of litigants as opposed to their representatives. He also came across as one indifferent to judicial politics. I was sure he knew more about mine than he let on. He was one of the few I did not seek to remove from either my case or the bench, having earned the unofficial status of Judge # 36.

This conference did not involve any family court warrant, but it did encompass the means for preventing it. The combined impact of multiple proceedings in diverse courts of jurisdiction at the time is too complicated for this short story. However, some background can be enlightening, maybe even intriguing from both a professional and lay person standpoint. So stay with me.

On November 4, 2009, my life was forever altered when I learned that my secretary had been scheming with outsiders to tamper with mail, court appointments and mortgage obligations. She had been setting me up for ethics violations. I could not see this coming, and if it derailed me to a state of total confusion, I could not expect the reader to follow this chapter of my ongoing saga. But it is so mind-boggling that a good faith effort could prevent such a tragedy to another victim.

I fired this secretary upon learning of her scheme, but on the same day I also learned that she had pilfered bank accounts, impairing my ability to satisfy a support debt created under protest with a reserve fund among those accounts. Her audacity could only be explained by an association with influential outsiders. Nevertheless, I promptly reported her crimes but was quickly advised from connections in law enforcement that I should back off until all my ducks were in order.

As it was explained in confidence, I was the target with my secretary as a possible witness who was offered prosecutorial immunity. This elevated my ordeal to a level that would overwhelm any average person. Now faced with a potential criminal concoction, every day became a high profile arrest waiting to happen. To be sure, it caused another lawyer in my office, similarly victimized, to seek professional assistance and a temporary departure from the practice of law.

My law license was consequently suspended for non-payment of child support three months later. But on August 23, 2010, an agreement was negotiated with the ex and her lawyer, then approved by a state supreme court judge (trial court of general jurisdiction). This agreement was arranged to satisfy child support arrears caused by all this misfortune. It was also intended to remove the license suspension so I could have the means to satisfy a revised payment plan.

The support violation was therefore removed, and the relieving order sent to both licensing courts of the upstate Appellate Division for reinstatement purposes. [34] This opened the door for the Fourth

---

[34] Unlike other states which vest licensing authority in their highest courts, New York has apportioned attorney regulation among four Departments of its middle level appeals courts known as the Appellate Division. They are located in Manhattan, Brooklyn, Albany and Rochester in that order. The author here was licensed in 1986 and first suspended by the Rochester court for support arrears on February 5, 2010. On November 27, 2009, he moved for disqualification of that court after being denied a motion directed to the misconduct of ethics lawyers. Discovered evidence could have necessitated a dismissal of trumped-up charges. The motion was also based on a federal court action filed earlier that year challenging disciplinary targeting. That motion was denied without prejudice but mysteriously granted on the court's own initiative on April 28, 2010 despite its suspension order issued between these dates. All litigation was then transferred to the Third Department which presided over the next ten years of reinstatement denials. Those years included the discharge of ethics lawyers in this witch hunt for falsifying time sheets and a series of inquiries chilling free speech, fn. 26. Although never disbarred, this author continues to suffer indefinite suspension from his peculiar treatment by two disciplinary courts of the same state.

Department court to lift the support suspension. Unfortunately, our objective was crushed by its sister court in the Third which was wrapping up a parallel ethics prosecution triggered by the same secretary. She had gone so far as to destroy proof needed for my defense. My cases were transferred there due to a rare order by agreement of the presiding justices.

The latter court ultimately issued suspension terms of one year, then six months based on events unearthed as far back as the 1990s. There were too many flaws in this process which verified its witch hunt nature. For example, one grievance was withdrawn for its falsity. Already in my ethics file, the sponsor was still forced to testify to its orchestration at my disciplinary hearing. Another was not even given the standard right of reply, and a third was instigated by lawyers who took over one of my cases. As karma would go, they were later prosecuted for contempt as I predicted. In the end, this case was dismissed, killing a promising settlement. [35]

Both terms were completed in 2013, but the latter transferee court denied all reinstatement thereafter. The regularly asserted fact that my secretary was behind it all did not matter. The 2010 support agreement did not matter either. It should have ended all the turmoil. Unfortunately, not only was the systemic retaliation and internal crimes complicated, but I was also made subject to an antiquated, 11-trial court structure in the underlying litigation. It yielded off-the-charts chaos.

This is not a self-serving claim, but a serious dysfunction backed by a 2017 state bar report that compared New York's structure to the single trial court of our largest state of California having twice the population. That report was generated to promote reform at

---

[35] <u>Brown v City of Syracuse</u>, 623 F. Supp.2d 272 (NDNY 2009); <u>Brown v Syracuse</u>, 673 F.3d 141 (2nd Cir. 2012)

a constitutional convention rejected by voters after vigorous union opposition. [36] Contemporaneous excerpts are revealing:

> *Whether New Yorkers are seeking a divorce and child support, challenging a speeding ticket, resolving a business dispute or serving on a jury, they must negotiate a complex and baffling state court system... It is so complicated that Article VI of the state Constitution requires more than 15,000 words to describe it. In contrast, the Judiciary Article of the U.S. Constitution is only 375 words... It (New York Constitution) is a 52,500 word behemoth filled with minutia and obsolete provisions, and even sections that the U.S. Supreme Court has declared unconstitutional.*

This glaring structural flaw was sufficient of itself to raise due process violations. Like a Fed Ex driver, I was being sent to various trial courts, one that featured a 160-mile round trip to receive a decision that had already been completed. Along the way, more than forty trial level jurists were assigned, a national record by most accounts. Worse yet, the combined chaos was enough to confound most experts, all the more appealing to the wrongdoers because this would foreclose accountability by scaring off any reporter or oversight agent. It was pure harassment on steroids.

That harassment was further joined by a support collection agency which violated our support order under the fiction of an acquired tax lien. Supposedly this made it a non-party even though it was acting contrary to that status. My children were not public charges, so there was certainly no taxpayer interest. If anything, this agency was acting in contempt of court through its harmful assistance, prompting litigation that would be blamed on me, the one honoring that order.

---

[36] NYSBA News Release, June 19, 2017: NYS Bar Association Supports a Constitutional Convention to Restructure the NYS Judiciary, Enhance Voter Participation and Modernize and Streamline the NYS Constitution

To prevent such corruption from succeeding altogether, and to raise justification for a federal investigation, additional disclosure is needed. The 2010 agreement called for a sale of my home to satisfy any future arrears upon a two-month delinquency. In that event, excess proceeds would be put in a trust account to cover child support for many years. This, in turn, would prevent more filings, a laudable objective for any judge including the one who signed the approving order. In it, he logically prohibited other asset seizures to make our revised payment plan work.

Without any such delinquency, the agreement was violated only two months later when this agency seized automobiles needed for employment. And it wasn't just any seizure but a sting operation resembling a drug bust. My home was never sold. Instead, over the next ten years, I was repeatedly hauled into family court which lacked jurisdiction over the real estate. What it did have was the power to incarcerate me over those same arrears which it aggressively pursued. If true justice and judicial economy prevailed, a scheming ex-wife would have been transferred to the proper court. That logic was tested before Judge Paris, but it is better left for a later chapter.

This fixation to cage me only yielded more harm to innocent persons. My ex-secretary became so empowered that she opened her own practice. For years, she represented unsuspecting clients in various courts, completing entire divorce cases without a license. No one acted upon my 2012 internal report delivered to the district attorney and city police department which contained a series of sworn statements and supporting documents behind her crime spree and prediction of her crimes upon later law office employers. I was referred instead to the lunacy of civil recourse.

That all changed when this ex-secretary was arrested the next year on a tip phoned in to a judge of an a nearby county where she was headed for a traffic court case. She was questioned by that judge, and after continued denials, was handcuffed in court on resulting criminal charges. She was later featured on our *Pretend Lawyer* website, saving at least one law firm in New Orleans from hiring her while on the run. It also showed how easily one could operate a divorce practice.

As for the ongoing support fiasco, it was a dispute settled by private parties and the only two (fit) parents of the subject children. If parental agreement approved by a state supreme court judge was unreliable, then why go to court at all? Such forums were created for the very purpose of preventing people from taking the law into their own hands. When justice is brazenly sabotaged, violence is a natural consequence as we have seen in recent years. But that's New York for you.

Judge Paris was seeking to resolve as much of this chaos as his jurisdiction would allow. At the time, he was presiding over a mortgage foreclosure action upon my home, the only major asset remaining for support satisfaction now that other means had collapsed during the witch hunt. That action was filed in 2012 after my law practice was necessarily closed for the same reason. The foreclosure ended in 2018 with an order made subject to a confidentiality clause. I can state, however, that I remain as owner and occupant of that home without mortgage obligation.

When Judge Paris learned of my location, he must have suspected my game plan to avoid a pending arrest warrant for support delinquencies that were also a subject of his foreclosure case. In any event, he told me to take whatever time I needed for whatever business brought me to Paris. The bank's pretrial motion to remove me from my home would be put off until I returned.

<u>Bull in a China Closet</u>

Lora called shortly afterward, and I told her about my fateful phone chat. I also reminded her of my ex-secretary. Three years prior to her discharge, I was making a formal announcement to run for state senate. Recently separated, I sought to make a good public image by having Lora join me at the news conference with my eldest daughter. What a great future for my children, but the ex would have none of it, and the secretary threw a tantrum when Lora arrived in professional attire. Together the two scorned women took aim like the proverbial *bull in a china closet*.

This secretary had gotten the false impression somehow that, as my campaign manager, she would be featured alongside me instead. I resolved the issue but not the true cause, a festering fatal attraction which factored into the evil she hatched afterward. Lora recalled the incident. She also played her part as intended at the conference but could not relate to the criminal enterprise which eventually landed the ex-secretary in jail, a sociopath raised without any father figure. [37]

"Hey, Lora, you'll never believe what just happened here in Paris," I opened with a chuckle.

"Your ex fell off the Eiffel Tower?"

Lora asked her question, as she typically did, with the driest sense of humor. Sometimes it was difficult to tell when she was serious. Then she might keep at it with my confused reactions until an entire conversation could be completed with a lighter side to life.

"In my dreams, maybe. I should've thrown her off. To think I had that opportunity once."

"Now I'm glad you chose her over me. That's not the honeymoon I

---

[37] Patrick Corbett, *Koziol Switches Campaigns*, Observer Dispatch, April 12, 2006

had in mind, Leon. An 'I-do' at the alter followed by an 'I did' skydiving from the Eiffel Tower. At least give me a parachute. Not very romantic."

"Neither is Paris today, Lora. You have no idea. I'm still being persecuted for free speech here, by inter-continental phone no less. But you know you could've prevented it all, don't you?"

"How was I supposed to that? I don't know any mafia guys."

"Who needs mafia? Remember that party at my home, your nasty encounter before Kelly and I got married. You were going to throw her into my fireplace if memory serves me correct."

"Yeah, I remember that. She chose to push me, and I chose to burn her at the stake. That's fair, isn't it? I mean that's what we do to witches. And to think, you invited me, enjoying it all."

"How could I resist, a front row seat to a catfight. Besides, you accepted that invite."

"You should've invited a psychiatrist. What was Kelly thinking with her energizer-bunny filings? Was she hell bent on destroying your career just to get revenge? Seriously now, how could a high school teacher bite the hand that was feeding her, not to mention your girls?"

"She did it with an onslaught of lies, but judges seemed to love her for it. Never did they scold her even after all her offense petitions were thrown out. She drew first blood by filing for more money, and that forced me to defend and show how I was being alienated for that money. You're lucky you never had children. The more you love them, the more you will spend with a motive to lie. Perjury is not enforced because it would fill our jails. Good parents are being turned into criminals while absentees run carefree. That's why I tell everyone to stay out of these courts."

"And that's why they came at you so hard. You hit them in their wallets. So sad after all you built for your girls. Okay, enough with Pinocchio, so what happened, a French maid catch you in the shower?

You know you left your room unlocked with a service request on the outside door."

"Very funny. A Judge Paris in Syracuse called me here in Paris."

"That's it? Breaking news for the day? Now I'm gonna jump off that tower. Am I baking a cake for a prison break-out or not? That's what I wanna know. I'm still looking for a chisel."

"Forget the chisel. The cake might be all you need the way you bake. I lost a few teeth trying your handiwork. Actually, Lora, he called about my ex-secretary's handiwork."

"Handiwork? Try dental work? A regular tooth monster, and I never even baked her a cake."

"Yeah, that's right, jagged jaws. Imagine a guy trying to kiss that?"

"There are worse things a guy might do with that mouth." I could picture Lora rolling her eyes.

"Anyway, Judge Paris might not enforce that loan she forged in my name. The child support will be put off with it because he has jurisdiction over both matters which family court does not."

"Now you're nauseating. Stop with the legalese. That's good news, right?"

"It seems so, but there are multiple judges involved. Some of them who hung out with me did the right thing by stepping off my case. Still, I'm sure there's all sorts of scrambling behind the scenes especially after John posted his latest hate crime against judges on my website. He's supposed to be covering for me during my wonderful vacation here."

"You mean the same John who throws you in the ring, telling you how great you look all bloodied up from this crusade? Then he watches like a kid from the nosebleed section?"

"Yeah, that John. He calls me Rocky every time I head to family court."

"You're Rocky alright heading for a boxing match at the county lock-up."

"Thanks Lora, you could've humored me on the last one. I'm a fugitive now, remember?"

"Sorry, just doing my best to cheer you up."

"I'm all cheered up now. Don't know what I'd do if you weren't checking on me every day."

"You mean no one else has called all this time in Paris?"

"Well, Mike Brancaccio did, but not for my sake. He's facing an arrest warrant for child support like me. It's only several thousand dollars, but his was officially issued, by the same family judge no less. I told him they were going to find him one way or another in the states. They'll extradite him to serve time. He couldn't believe his own lawyer may be facing the same thing in Paris."

"Well, then, that makes you his *Cousin Vinny*, right?"

"You just can't stop, can you?"

"Sorry again. I remember Mike. A nice guy but always in trouble. Is he coming out to join you?"

"He can't without a passport, and they won't issue one with the warrant on the sheriff website. Hey that's Mike calling me right now. What's the chance of that? Let me get back to you Lora."

"Sure, no problem. But be careful. I need you to come back and try my new cake recipe."

If It Don't Bend, You Can't Contend

Among cases I litigated over the past quarter century, Mike Brancaccio was a foolish teen when he first came to my law office during the nineties. He was charged with a gang assault upon two influential victims, a city police officer and a legislative aide to former New York

Senate Leader Joseph Bruno whose autobiography is referenced in Chapter One. For that reason, the case was widely considered to be one that would be impossible to win. But that was before the abuses of a police badge and public office which I exposed during trial.

Both injured complainants were invited to a house party in east Utica, a neighborhood known for its gang fights and mafia lore. Trying to show off to the girls hosting this party, the officer directed Mike and his friends to leave after some long forgotten commotion. They refused. The cop was off-duty, on leave for a disability and acting beyond any scope of authority when he sprung out his badge to enforce that directive.

In response, Mike knocked the badge out of the cop's hand, believing it was not genuine. It prompted a scuffle. The cop's friend (legislative aide) then made the mistake of jumping into the fray. Under rules of engagement in this rough neighborhood, when someone interrupts a fair fight, it's open season for a brawl not a peace treaty. Anything goes.

And that's what happened, eventually spilling out into the streets. A gang assault on both followed, resulting in serious injuries and hospitalization of the cop and friend, both claiming to be there at the request of party hosts when the directives were made. Despite a thorough beating and escape to the cop's home across the street, the pounding continued on his front porch before a successful retreat could be completed.

During the jury trial, deliberations were highly skewed against Mike who believed, along with his parents, that he was being prejudiced due to his Italian-American heritage. The better explanation was that he was being set up for a conviction due to the status of his victims. This played out time and again during heated exchanges and objections that were routinely denied by the presiding judge whenever I made them for whatever reasons.

My professional responsibility to a client I barely knew became more challenging when I returned from a lunch recess to discover a set of bloody clothes on the witness stand only a few feet away from the jury box. I promptly sought out the judge in chambers to order their immediate removal but was advised that a decision would be made once he resumed the bench. By that time, the jury would return, as it did, and the intended effect was achieved.

This calculated delay obviously diluted the value of my motion to remove those clothes. It was belatedly granted on grounds that their prejudicial effect outweighed any evidentiary value. The mother of the legislative aide nevertheless provided the gory details at the start of afternoon proceedings. Her son had been hit over the head with a bottle causing stitches to the scalp.

It was looking even worse for the defense when the police officer took the stand. He explained how Mike had thrown him over the porch rail when trying to escape inside his own home. To accent a disrespect for law enforcement, he testified that Mike did much more than slap down a police badge. His version had Mike grabbing the badge, bending it and throwing it back into the officer's face. At that point, the faces of our jury looked like Mike would need his toothbrush.

But like so many things in my life that turned on a daring move, I asked the off-duty cop to show us that badge. He removed it from his wallet and proudly displayed the item before the spectators in the courtroom. They included legislative observers and prosecution assistants. To their dismay, I asked to examine that badge. I don't recall if there was any objection, it had not been offered into evidence, but he handed it over to me anyway from the witness stand.

At great risk, I attempted to bend the badge to no avail. I turned and attempted it again where everyone could see it. Most knew where I was going with this but could not know how far. I offered to publish it and have the jurors try to bend the same item. This judge did not want to permit any such experiment, but to deny it would be to demonstrate that justice and truth-seeking were not his objectives. My repeated motions for a mistrial had already been denied.

Indeed, during one volatile exchange in chambers, the judge complained that he had never been subjected to so many challenges to his impartiality. Nevertheless, I was able to cast reasonable doubt on the issue of intent behind any assault of Joe Bruno's aide. Mike testified that he had pulled his friends off him after finishing his fight with the cop. But unless I could show consistent physical engagement, self-defense was untenable after his pursuit across the street.

The tide turned finally in our favor when the prosecution called the girl who hosted this party to the stand. She gave a rendition of events leading up to the fight but not much more. I had been tipped off that the off-duty cop returned from his apartment after the fight ended with a gun. He brandished it in order to get her to reveal the names of his assailants.

I cross examined her with a risky question which would be deemed a very desperate one if she denied the gun incident. Fortunately, she candidly disclosed that it did happen, and by all indications, the prosecution was unaware of this.

Now everything changed as I was able to elicit a conclusion opposite that which had been contended by the prosecution all along, that it was the cop and not my client showing disrespect for law enforcement and public safety. And it occurred right before the eyes of judge and jury.

Michael Brancaccio was acquitted in less than forty-five minutes. None of this made big time news. After all, he was only a teen punk from east Utica being falsely accused. But had he been a famous actor and football star for the Buffalo Bills, a tight glove would pale in comparison. In the O.J. Simpson case one year later, a high powered legal team decried: "If it don't fit, you got to acquit." In our case, the pitch had already been made: "If it don't bend, you can't contend."

After the unexpected verdict, the prosecutor stormed out, not even a handshake. I followed with a civil rights action against the Utica police department resulting in a decent recovery. Mike was effectively rewarded for beating up a cop while others in the fracas took guilty pleas. The city presiding judge was Anthony Garramone whose wife and sister I had successfully represented on unrelated matters. The losing district attorney of a can't-miss case was Scott McNamara.

Scott became the county's top prosecutor years later, refusing to indict my secretary for crimes in my law office. For years she was given a free pass, maybe even prosecutorial immunity until, as predicted in my 2012 report, her empowerment led to that unlawful practice. At the same time, she was reaping havoc as a newly hired secretary for our district's ethics chairman. Yes, it was all too bizarre, an ordeal for the ages, one befitting a Rod Serling narrative in the Twilight Zone.

To be sure, Utica police were doing their part on this show, refusing to arrest the same secretary on my complaints. Instead, they referred me to civil recourse as if she had the means to return six figures in stolen money. When finally sent to jail on forgery convictions in 2016, her victims were interstate and growing by the month. By that year, my law license had been suspended for over six years due to my inability to prove crime victim status in reinstatement proceedings.

Mike was eventually jailed for six months on the support warrant issued by Family Judge Daniel King, twice the three month sentence given to my ex-secretary on each of two felony counts. His mom called me, complaining that her son was accosted by King in court due to the money spent for his lawyer which could have been applied to the support debt. Like so many fathers, Mike was in a recurring cycle of judicial abuse and imprisonment while his debt continued to grow.

Most support victims and the public generally are unaware that monthly support obligations continue to accrue while a debtor is incarcerated for any reason. It's just another aspect of the revenue design at the true heart of this custody system. Upon release, the debt is insurmountable with accumulated interest and impaired employment. But judges know they can fleece extended families through draconian collection devices such as another warrant or jail commitment.

It has created a de facto debtor prison with no real difference from the one declared unconstitutional 200 years ago except that the state is now the debt collector with enforcement powers that would dwarf the capacity of any private entity. Through an orchestrated opinion of a judge in a self-regulated climate, discretion can easily be abused as it was here simply because a person appears offensive or gives public opinions critical of a judge.

Mike was now a displaced forty-year old. He relied on me in the worst of jams. But rather than follow my lead on the support warrant, he decided he was going to do the tough guy routine, thinking he could beat the system by serving time as a form of protest. No one cared. No one rallied for him. Support victims were too busy bowling, basket-balling and shopping instead.

Mike couldn't handle the hypocrisy, doing more time than violent felons. He was hospitalized after his release from Lewis County jail. Increasingly, these courts are producing PTSD like our foreign wars are. To avoid recurring jail terms, Mike gave up his parent rights. The ex promptly changed their daughter's last name to the one shared with her husband. The nine-year old girl would never hear from her daddy again. On October 11, 2020, he took his life at age forty-six.

As bizarre things would go, the "custodial parent" displayed the minimal conscience of bringing that nine-year old girl to Mike's funeral.

Not surprisingly she broke down crying at the sight of her dad in a coffin. I could verify the eternal connection she shared with him by the several chats on speaker phone that I overheard during our lobbying excursions. After composing herself, the little girl asked her mom whether her dad had died "because of all the court stuff."

CHAPTER 6

WEAVING A TANGLED WEB

When I finished my depressing conversation with Mike, I left Republic Square and searched for the first Irish Pub I could find. During my time in Paris, I struggled to locate eating establishments offering the kind of meals I enjoyed back home. Not a spicy food connoisseur, I craved the bland. Give me some corned beef and cabbage, or a hearty stew and salad, and I'm a happy camper. Polish, German or Irish dinners were the best as far as my palate was concerned.

I also enjoyed conversation at a bar over a couple of Budweisers before eating. But what I routinely found in this city were restaurants where they seated you at a table, in my case a tiny two-seater in the corner or cramped between larger tables with groups happily conversing. I got more than a few disgusted looks thrown my way. Maybe it was because I was American, but the better view is that singles were outcasts. If there was a bar, it might be an aluminum stand-up counter with no stools.

That wasn't nearly the aggravation experienced when a coronavirus would ravage the world years later, but I managed to find refuge at the Irish pubs. They were my oases. One in the city's Fourth Arrondissement became my home away from home. Known as Corcoran's, it was located only a few blocks east of Bastille Plaza at 53 Rue du Faubourg Saint-Antoine.

In fair proximity to major sites at city center, the district here also featured some of the best night clubs in all of Paris. They could be found along narrow, brick or cobble streets, a throw-back to the city's medieval times. Near Bastille monument, there were also quaint establishments of sufficient variety to accommodate all interests.

Whether he was a bartender, manager or owner, Sean was a fellow dad who hit it off with me from the moment we met. He opened with the usual greetings for a tourist mecca, exploring my reasons for being in Paris. But it wasn't long before conversation expanded, not the typical kind, but one surrounding my visits to human rights agencies.

We quickly became comrades upon sharing his own divorce experiences. Evidently this custody regime had inflicted all sorts of chaos in France, Ireland, the UK and other western nations. I cemented that conclusion as soon as patrons and staff overheard my reasons for being at this watering hole. They could not get enough of my stories, not to mention all the free advice. Before you knew it, we were making plans for a world headquarters for my Parenting Rights Institute.

During another dinner stop here, I was treated to real entertainment after a wholesome meal. The singers, fiddles and jigs were straight out of Ireland, only a short flight across the English Channel. It was also on this day that I met a single mom who was in the heat of a custody battle in the states. I was at it again when a group of parents were exchanging multi-nation divorce scandals with me at the bar. This mom managed to whittle it all down to an exclusive conversation.

Her name was Linda, and she wore a brown, plaid skirt with white blouse, smiling in a manner that drew you seductively into her world. Slender with long, jet-black hair curled around one of her shoulders, she could not have been much taller than five feet. Seated on a stool to my right, she was overtly nervous, eyes wandering at times, her legs crossed and switching them regularly.

"So, Mr. big-shot New York lawyer, what do you know about French custody law? I need a court order against my ex in California. Can I pick your brain or is there going to be a fee for this?"

"My, you're so subtle. Before I answer though, I'm going to have to frisk you. How do I know you're not some undercover agent eavesdropping? And stop with the formalities. My friends call me Lee. Just to set the record straight, I'm no big-shot, more like I got shot big-time. Let's call it an assassination by my own profession. Why do you ask?"

"Well I overheard you talking with the guys a little while ago about some casino you shut down in New York. It's obvious you were showing off after dumping on the bartender about family court corruption. It's just what they wanted to hear to bring on their own war stories. Is that how you troll for clients back home? It didn't fool me."

"So subtle again! There goes the free ride on that advice. To answer your real question though, that shut-down never happened. I did what my landowner clients hired me to do. I got the decision which was supposed to make it close, but like custody and divorce, money talks. The casino's still there. An Indian land claim basically paid for it before that was thrown out."

"No surprise there, but impressive enough, so you still must be good at what you do."

"Depends how you look at it, very complicated. I mean they flew in lawyers from as far away as Washington to argue against me. One of the law firms was Cravath, Swaine and Moore. You should see their office building near Times Square. But they did an end-around using federal authority over Indian affairs, eventually rewarded with a valid casino and land in trust but only a fraction of the six million acres originally demanded. So you could say I won and lost at the same time."

"For a lone wolf, that's still impressive. But it's all too much to digest, way beyond my pay grade. So why are you acting like a local then? Why not just set up a law practice here?"

"I'm a bit intrigued by your questions. We barely know each other. I thought your custody case was in the United States. What do you care about French law and a practice for me in Paris?"

"Let's just say my issues cross the borders. I may end up subject to custody laws here, but they're not in my favor. I paid good money for the best lawyers to make sure my child was safe under my care. Now I'm finding that my abusive ex is going to have him seized and returned."

"Huh, that's strange. From what I've read, France has a maternal preference in such matters. That seems to prevail even though it's part of the European Union which stresses that both parents and their children have a right to a relationship. So I would think you'd be happy here. In the states, dads are nearly 85% of parents paying child support. You should be good there too."

"Well, my case is unique. It goes far beyond basic custody laws."

"How so?"

"It involves international law. Leave it at that. When I heard you talking about sovereignty issues with Sean, I figured you might be just the right guy for my case."

"Again, I think you misunderstood what we were talking about. I got off on the Native-American sovereignty claims which seem to fascinate Europeans. They used it to get that casino compact. But they have their own custody norms, very sophisticated, nothing that could apply to you."

"Maybe, maybe not. Do you have a business card? I'd like to give you my whole story on the phone, maybe over some early morning expresso if you don't mind. Right now, it's too noisy at this pub. That's why I didn't pick up on all of what you were saying."

"Sure, no problem," I replied while handing her my advocacy card. "Maybe I'll regret this but just call me a risk-taker. You know it's just bar talk. Don't get too pumped by the beer muscles."

"Got it. So now, getting away from the shop talk, what do you like to do for fun?"

"Well, I like skiing, swimming, mountain climbing and dodging my parole officer."

"What?"

"Lighten up. I'm kidding. Just thought I'd throw in a little humor on our first date."

"Oh is that what this is now?" she asked while pulling her stool up closer to mine. "You can give me all the free advice you want, but I'm not going to bed with you."

She made her announcement with an alluring smile, no exclamation point, more like a comma. Her body language was much more convincing.

"Hey, you can't blame me for trying. Take it as a compliment, but I really wasn't expecting sex. Maybe on our next date."

Linda smiled with a more serious look now while taking a sip from her drink. Then she grimaced. Reaching for my shirt collar, she drew me close before whispering, "from the moment you crushed on me, I knew you would play me at some point. Now you're doing just that. Even though I wasn't born yesterday, sometimes 'no' means 'yes,' that is if you really are a risk-taker."

That comment truly caught me off guard. She must have picked up on my glances during the group exchanges. Demurring to her conclusions, I continued to trade vital information for multiple reasons with no conception of time or place. It became quite arousing, if not romantic.

Over the years, I had been dealing with victims electronically for the most part. As fate would have it, this would prepare me for a pandemic that would soon make its devastating impact. Deeper into our conversation, I learned that Linda was a crusader like me who had taken on more than her parenting rival. She had taken aim at corruption in the California divorce system, generating reports to various commissions, monitoring court proceedings and organizing rallies against domestic violence. In the end, she came up with essentially the same conclusions I did.

She related an ordeal that could be considered my maternal counterpart even with some puzzle pieces missing. Occasionally melancholy, she betrayed great wit and broke out laughing at her own jokes. She was a verbal gladiator, caretaker, intellectual, airhead, control freak and hopeless romantic all rolled up into one. She may have lit up the DSM-5 manual, and all the more sexy for it, bringing reminders of actress Debra Messing, a/k/a Kat in the acclaimed film, *Wedding Date*.

Yes, you could say that chance had brought another eclectic personality into my ever changing world, one that I desperately needed right now, a jump start of sorts even if it did add to my risks. That much was accentuated whenever our discourse returned to child custody. A familiar dark side would show up in her, a veritable Jeckle-Hyde figment in the flesh. A deep-seated hatred for this corrupted system had locked onto our meeting. Visions of my ex-secretary began surfacing.

As our discourse continued to grow more trusting into the night, band music faded, loud patrons along with it. I could sense that something special was developing between us. In a matter of hours, total strangers had been transformed into kindred spirits, fate-driven partners on a mission to save our offspring from common enemies thousands of miles apart.

After becoming more intimate, I invited Linda out for a stroll. I'd seen enough romantic couples arm-in-arm on these streets during my nightly returns to the hotel. Anxious to get a taste, it was a chance I took. To my delight, Linda eagerly accepted. After satisfying a bar tab which could rival a lease payment, we exited Corcoran's to join the evening glitz and a lover's side to Paris.

We headed back toward Place de la Bastille which was teeming with activity, from late diners seated outside various cafes to diverse tourists engaged in dialogue of many languages. You couldn't help wondering how all that meshed in one place without conflict or collision. We took photos of one another, then together at the urging of an elderly couple on an anniversary honeymoon. With their well wishes, we were suddenly on an impromptu honeymoon of our own.

One street off the northeast side of the plaza was quite inviting. We sauntered aimlessly along Rue de la Roquette, pausing from time to time to investigate the boutiques which caught Linda's eye. Then we turned right onto Rue de Lappe as the passages narrowed. Here we found clubs galore and a hoard of night-goers which might intimidate many older tourists. To us it was an unexpected adventure, a trip back in time, a foray into our long-lost youth.

For no particular reason except its peculiar name, we boldly entered a night club known as *Yellow Mad Monkey*. Lots of energy inside, and there were even large plants suspended from the ceiling to give this place a sort of jungle décor. Tarzan himself might swing down for a beer. There were several chairs at a long table that seemed available, maybe the only ones in this crowded venue, but the two couples already seated there appeared to have claimed title to them.

We must have looked out of place because, sensing our predicament, one of the guys motioned us over. His name was Pierre from Quebec City, Canada, and after we seated ourselves, he politely introduced us to his wife, Charlene, and acquaintances, Hank and Sheila. The latter couple hailed from West Virginia and the foursome had met at the Louvre earlier in the week. None of us being locals, it was easy to join their conversation over tourist sites.

"So what brings you two to Gay Paree?" our spontaneous host eventually asked. Pierre was a tall, buffed fellow in grey slacks and black silk shirt, middle aged with a Toby Keith goatee.

"Oh we're on our honeymoon, second marriage," Linda replied with convincing character. She directed a celebratory smile toward each of our table mates and earned the intended reactions. Once again, I was taken aback but caught on quickly. We were going to have some fun with this, a role which that elderly couple assigned to us a short while ago and see where it all went.

"That's so nice. Such a loving couple, you guys, don't you think Pierre?" Charlene was a shapely woman dressed in black pants and sky-blue top. A pearl necklace, jewelry on both hands, and high end cosmetics, she exuded success. "I remember our honeymoon in Niagara Falls. So long ago, seems like yesterday," she mused. "Where did all that time go?"

"I say we all get a shot and toast your new life together." The offer came from Sheila, a long time girlfriend of Hank, the third man at our table. He was a burly guy dressed casually in jeans and a Mountaineers jersey evidently suffering from a sight defect because he could not seem to keep his eyes off Linda's chest. Sheila came across as a fun-loving type, curvy figure and bleach blonde hair caught up in a bun. A red dress matched her rosy cheeks, and her arms were sufficient to scare Rambo away.

"Sure, why not, but I don't do shots," I answered. "Turned down enough of them at our wedding. Thanks anyway. I'll just substitute with a bottle of Bud. How about you, honey?"

Linda was immediately ecstatic with my play-along, aggressively looking for excitement the way a child explores a carnival.

"I'll have a vodka cranberry instead darling. We've had a long day, Sheila, and I can't wait to get back to our room."

"Yeah, I know what ya mean. Damn Paris boulevards, they're so long and the sites way too far apart. We had to walk all day just to visit a few of them, and I'm ready to pass out."

"Uh, well, that's not what I meant. It's all that wild sex we've been getting, just can't get enough fast enough. So the last thing I intend to do is pass out like last night on the elevator. Another one of our quickies you know. And those tropical drinks at the hotel lounge didn't help."

Linda's remark caused me to burst out with a laugh. So unexpected, it's the way she delivered it. I guess you had to be there. I contained myself as soon as I lost it, then added, "And to think you were buck-naked when I took you off that elevator. Lucky for us, those heels of yours made a great door jam. We should try our room once in awhile, don't you think?"

"Okay babes, no date rape tonight, but why wait? You keep rubbing my thigh, and if you get much farther up my skirt, it's going to be fireworks for sure." Linda glanced around to gauge reactions. Unsatisfied with whatever she was instigating, she got bolder. "I don't think there's room under this table for another quickie. Should we try a stall in the ladies room?"

"Sure beats those conjugal visits at Rikers Island," I answered. "How could I have survived all that prison time without your trust in me? Charlene's right about us being a loving couple."

We kept alternating our fictions to a point where our new friends started reacting with squint- eyes and strange looks toward us and then each other. Linda was flawless, but I was sure I could make her dam burst despite the composure she needed for her ruse, where ever that was going.

"Sorry guys, but we've been doing this foreplay all evening. We should've let you in more casually and gotten to know you better. So what about you guys? Has this been the romantic city we hear so much about? Any action yet Charlene? Niagara Falls can't be that far away?"

There was no reaction from Charlene. She just looked back at Linda unsure of her reply. Linda was obviously getting quite loopy and carried away. But she could never have predicted what would follow, taking us both over the falls here.

Concededly this was a foursome that was hard to read, square peg in a round hole, a classy, reserved couple touring with Bonnie and Clyde. But give Linda credit, she was determined. On the chance she offended anyone, she tried to make amends. Unfortunately, she overcompensated.

"I mean, we're here to have a love adventure, a wild time together, aren't we? We were just trying give you guys some inspiration. So is it gonna be group sex tonight or not?"

Linda was obviously joking and meant a foursome, but she never got her anticipated response. What she did get was a game changer. Sheila seized the moment as group representative. "Well I don't see why that can't be arranged now that you offer it. Last night we got some at the Palace Suite where Pierre and Charlene are staying. You should see the place, a huge balcony overlooking the city and some sex toys that Hank and I brought along from our own hotel."

Linda could never have imagined what her misconstrued offer would trigger. Neither could I. But it's something we would never forget. Now producing our own confused silence, Sheila pressed on with a fantasy trip of her own, one that was no ruse.

"Hey, whatever you two got going on, I wanna be a part of it. Did you hear that guys? Linda says she wants to share, like we all did last night. And what a night! Honey, you won't crash on my watch, and as for your man, he ain't seen nothing yet. You're gonna love our toys."

Sheila's version of x-rated far exceeded ours. It was shocking enough, but we were blown away when the other three at our table nodded approvingly. Linda and I were now their prey. It had to be an ambush. Neither of us could utter a word. How were we going to get out of this jam?

They were all looking so serious, no joking here, and for a moment I think Linda was feeling like she would actually be checking into the Hotel California. We stared in wonder, glanced at each another, our thoughts racing for a quick exit strategy. Then I decided on one.

"Sheila, you're on." I scribbled a room number on the back of a hotel card and handed it to her. "Try our palace, it's even more romantic. Bring your hottest nighty. And Hank, I got a cure for your eye problem, it's called gasoline. Right now, we gotta go and check out this porn shop."

I grabbed Linda by the hand and rushed her out of the club like *mad monkees*. That's when her dam finally burst. Laughing hysterically, she stumbled alongside me down the sidewalk. It wasn't long before we disappeared inconspicuously among the crowded streets.

When we got comfortable with our escape, Linda stopped, turned toward me and seized my elbows with each hand. She had that wide-eyed shock plastered all over her face. It was as if she was suddenly back in school after completing some kind of dare or sorority prank.

"I can't believe what just happened," she screamed, laughing to tears. "Tell me that didn't just happen. Did they really think we were looking for some kind of double manage-et-trois?"

"Not we, you! I never offered anything, certainly not an orgy. I think they call it swingers."

"Yeah, like you weren't enjoying it."

"Actually I was, right up to the point where it got real, when Bubba from the back woods was getting ready to join the fun. I gotta say, Lynn, you are crazy! I never met anyone quite like you."

"Same here, I never met someone like me either," she answered with a giggle. Then we locked our arms again and resumed our aimless stroll.

"I really like you, Lee the lawyer. You got me out of a real jam there. The bouncer is probably looking for us right now. We never did pay for our drinks. I could use help like that. Can we get together tomorrow night?"

"Sure, but before we do, isn't there a porn shop around here we're supposed to check out?"

Linda laughed aloud once again. "Besides," I added, "I gotta hope you're not too messed up right now. You downed a lot in only a few hours and might forget this whole thing even happened in the morning. Are you sure you're okay?"

"Absolutely, I'm getting good at this. A great stress reliever with all of what I've been going through. I got this lawyer right now who's acting like a scared boy in front of my custody judge."

"Well, then, it's obvious you hired the wrong lawyer. Protecting a child is a man's job, love."

Linda quickly wrapped her arms around my head, inflicting a French kiss like I had never experienced before. "Wild sex could be the icing on our wedding cake tonight. Whatta ya say?"

"Tempting as that is, let me take a raincheck for now. It's been a long day. Can I get you a cab, walk you home? I can't just leave you here."

"Aw that's so sweet. A real gentleman. Are you falling for me, Lee? I sensed a bit of jealousy, you know, back at that Monkee club. Gasoline? …. Seriously? Couldn't you come up with something more masculine, like, I'll knock you on your ass if you even peek at my wife's boobs again? Now that would have been a kick-ass reality check."

"You noticed it too, huh? Hey, the guy was a pervert, Lynn, and who knows what he might've been packing? After all, he never said a word all night, just kept staring at your breasts. Talk about mad monkees. I swear this one couldn't formulate words. Besides, how's a newlywed husband supposed to act? Good show by the way. You sure know how to take a guy off-guard."

"Well, I gotta say, you did rise to the occasion, and bonus, some real romance thrown in. I must admit, I'm not used to that. So glad we got married on our first date. Never had a wild ride like this, although I'm sure there are many others that have in this city."

"Thank goodness it wasn't a ride to some backwoods cabin with Hank and Sheila. Didn't they star in some *Deliverance* sequel? What were you thinking? I had all I could do to keep up with your shenanigans. And how in the world did that foursome match up anyway?"

"I wondered the same thing. By the way, you didn't really give out your room card, did you?"

"I can't believe you'd even ask. It was one of many business cards I've been collecting during my extended stay. My reservation at the current place is up next week, and the card I gave is from the last one I stayed at. The number on the back is the basement weight room."

Linda laughed aloud, then stopped and faced me again, this time with a serious look. "Hey Lee, with what you just said, a great idea popped into my head."

"Please, not another one. No more role playing. I'm only good for one per century."

"No, I'm serious, hear me out. There's this villa on the Riviera which has become my second home. I only come to Paris on business, staying with relatives when I'm here. Why not visit me this weekend? Put off your next reservation. You'll love it down there."

The offer took me off guard again, far more than my previous experiences, this time with a dose of suspicion. But she made her pitch enthusiastically, and frankly I fell for it, if not her. The proverbial tumbleweed, what did it matter where I went?

"Wow, that's quite an offer. I've never been to the Riviera. Always wanted to visit though. This is so unexpected, enchanting even. Besides, staying on the move may be just what the doctor ordered, especially after that call I got from Judge Paris."

"Judge Paris?"

"Never mind, long story. Tell you what, the more I think about it, the more I like your idea. Let's get together tomorrow night. We'll meet at Corcoran's and talk about this some more."

"What's there to talk about? If it's about that fire I started at Monkee Club, I got more where that came from. And you look like a guy who could use more fun like that. At the same time, I could use a guy like you to save me when it happens. You gotta admit, Lee, we had a riot getting out."

"O, what a tangled web we weave when we first practice deceit."

"What are you talking about, Lee?"

"Never mind again, another long story. It's a quote from an old friend, a real old friend. Hey there's a cab, let's grab it." We hopped into the back seat and away we went.

"Two stops, Rue de Clery at Poissonniere and Montmartre," I announced.

"Oui, Monsieur."

"You sure you don't want to make it one stop, Lee?"

"I'm a gentleman, remember? I may end up in Paris forever. So we got lots of time to get to know one another. If it's going to happen, I want it to be special. And I think you're real special, unfortunately very drunk too."

"Alrighty then, bad for me, good for you." Linda had been slurring her words but continued to recompose herself as if accustomed to it. I did my best not to notice until she eased us down into the back seat and assumed a commanding position. Then she began to kiss, caress and stimulate me as if she had not had sex in a very long time. Come to think about it, neither had I.

To my amazement, an unexpected metamorphosis was occurring, a sweet transition from nightmare to fairy tale. We were two oppressed victims making our way to paradise without a care in the world. The cab driver lost sight of us in his rearview mirror and could only fantasize about our moans and maneuverings as he navigated the streets longer than necessary.

Eventually he came to a stop. Linda got herself together and exited while I monitored her walk toward some family home near the drop-off location she gave me for the cab driver. Barely onto the sidewalk, she turned, bent over, and blew me a kiss. I smiled back. Then she sauntered off to points unknown, her now wrinkled blouse draping off one side of a displaced skirt. Whatever was left of her hairstyle and make-up combined to give the appearance of a very cute zombie.

As the cab driver resumed his route toward my hotel, I reminisced about this extraordinary day. I did not know what to make of it, much less a woman who won my heart in so many ways. I may not have known much about my destiny, but I did know that I wanted more of Linda. Maybe it was that perfume, her special touch, the ambiance of Paris or that wild ride at the Bastille.

Then again, maybe she was spinning a web I had never seen before.

CHAPTER 7

SOULMATE ENCOUNTER

Ring, ring… ring, ring…ring, ring.

I enjoyed hitting the speed bag from time to time, but not like I would've enjoyed hitting the telephone right now in my hotel room. One thing that was nice about life as a tumbleweed, you didn't need an alarm clock most of the time.

Last I remember using one was back home prior to my departure from JFK. And now I remember asking the front desk for a wake-up call. That time had come. I grabbed the receiver and spared the rest of the unit from a flight out the window.

"Hello."

"This is your wake-up call Leone and, oh, a notification that your wife stopped by with some kind of important delivery. It's in an envelope here at the front desk. She's quite attractive I might add. Should I get you a cab?"

"Uh, yeah… I mean no, Amanda, not yet anyway. And did you say my wife?"

"That's what I said, Leone." Amanda was the front desk clerk and she employed the French pronunciation for my first name. "Looks like you guys made up. That's so nice to see these days. I knew you weren't comfortable here. Now you can return home. May I recommend flowers? I know a good place just a few blocks over."

Amanda took good care of me during my stay at the third hotel of my fugitive life. I guessed she probably felt sorry for me, not knowing what I was going through. She seemed to have that woman's intuition about someone displaying everything but confidence in his surroundings. From a genuine cup of American coffee to a good recommendation for a currency exchange, I was in good hands with her at my helm each day. I'd like to say we became friends.

She obviously felt rewarded by whatever had occurred this morning in the lobby. I could not wait to find out what was in store for me today. Yeah right. The problem with a fake wife and an ex-wife now in my life, I could not know which one might be the source for this mystery delivery. It could be another ambush for all I knew.

Maybe it was another prank by Linda, a love note brought by the postman. Or maybe it was an extradition notice from an Interpol agent. When you get beat up as much as I had been, paranoia becomes routine. It was also not comforting to know that the international police agency was headquartered here in France. I was fairly certain, however, that it had to do with Linda.

This was also my last day at the current hotel. Always on the move, my next one was a short but steep walk away. I did not relish lugging my belongings like a turtle straight up Montmartre, but my reservation for another week had been secured the night before, and it would expire by 2 p.m.

The new room managed to come up even smaller than the one I squeezed around. This was the economy routine which I now learned came with the territory of risky speech in the free world. I lumbered out of my twin bed and into the shower before packing and heading for the elevator.

At the front desk, Amanda was smiling more than usual, apparently still pleased with my marital reconciliation. I did my best to reciprocate but was still apprehensive about the envelope. I think Amanda was a bit curious herself because she could not get her attention off my hands and reactions when I removed the contents. I unfolded the note and it read:

My Darling Husband,

> *Rise and shine! Your round trip tickets for the TGV to Marseille are enclosed with a brief stop at Lyon. There's also a money voucher for your expenses and any hotel cancellation. Three hours, and we'll be in each other's arms again. I can't wait to see you, so hurry up!*

Lynn.

P.S. I told Amanda all about our make-up sex last night.

I was unaware of any make-up sex the night before because it is typically preceded by an argument, and Linda and I had not experienced that yet. Instead, our past few days had matured into an intimate relationship. Together nearly every waking moment since we met, we made it official during an overnight here this past Saturday. During that time, we visited Notre Dame, spent an entire afternoon at the Louvre Museum and even reached the top of the Eiffel Tower.

Amanda was happy with my reactions to this unexpected delivery. I did not say much about it but thanked her for being such a wonderful host. Then I took her up on the cab offer, relieved that I would not be climbing up any hill. Instead, although I had not officially taken Linda up on her offer, the decision was now made for me.

I sat down in the lobby after grabbing a cup of coffee and morning pastry while waiting for that cab. I could not help smiling again after re-reading Linda's note. This was some take-charge woman with an upbeat attitude. I wasn't used to that in my love life but loving it so far.

The cab ride was long but the train part remarkably fast. Only a few miles to the Paris train station, Gare de Lyon, but over 400 miles to Cote 'Azure, or the French Riviera from there. Unlike the states, European countries such as France are served by high speed rail that make buses, automobiles and, in some instances, even air travel obsolete.

The TGV, or Train 'a Grande Vitesse, set a record speed exceeding 350 miles per hour, and the one I was boarding was known to reach passenger speeds of 200. That would explain Linda's ETA of three hours to cover such a distance. At nearly four times the maximum speeds I was used to on the trains back home, the scenery flew by at such velocity that it was often difficult to focus on anything. The countryside was otherwise pastoral and the trip quite comfortable.

Linda was waiting for me at the station in Marseille. As soon as I stepped onto the platform, she ran over and jumped into my arms straddling my waist with her legs. She kissed me incessantly having no regard for other passengers making their way around us. I must admit neither did I.

After exchanging basic information, I secured my bags and followed her to a parking area where I unloaded into the trunk of a silver fiat. And then we were off to the other side of Nice along a winding coastal highway and my first view of the spectacular Riviera.

It took us a couple of hours to reach the eastern district but no matter, my attention was glued to the picturesque route. We by-passed the city of Nice ending up in a place called Cap-d' Ail. This is where Linda's villa was located on a hillside overlooking the beautiful aqua waters of the Mediterranean. We drove up the back side and came to a stop in a private driveway where I got out to look around.

I couldn't help but take a few moments aside for a breathtaking view.

There were several sailboats below and a super-yacht in the distance. This was a cape with an overlook, a sort of mini-Montmartre jutting out onto the sea. Yeah, I could stay here forever. Not a problem. Linda was exhibiting her own excitement to my reactions.

"Not too shabby, huh Lee?"

"Shabby? That's putting it mildly, try exquisite."

"Exquisite, I like that. I knew you were good at words. I think that's what I'll call the place, Cape Exquisite. Maybe it'll catch on."

"I'm so glad you invited me here."

"So glad you accepted. Never thought I would have to work overtime to get you to come to this idyllic haven. The place actually belongs to someone else, but he's elderly, childless, and his wife passed away last year. He's a successful tech investor from Hong Kong with his own IP firm. I took care of his patent issues during her final days, and this was my reward. He's pretty much abandoned the place. So you could say I own it unless he calls for a lease payment."

A stately residence with a gated entrance and balcony, the reddish tile roofing complemented other homes in the area. Inside everything was modern, black and white furnishings, a large living room, several bedrooms, two baths and a jacuzzi on the rear deck overlooking the sea.

Linda guided me into a guest room but would not let me get settled. Instead, she popped the cork of a bottle of French Champagne and poured us both a glass. Then she directed me to her deck where we engaged in a sort of toast to my arrival and a budding relationship.

Linda gave me an overview of her neighborhood, pointing to where the market, beaches and tourist attractions were. After a couple glasses, we returned inside where Linda escorted me by hand into the master bedroom. It was a luxurious one that she had every intention of exploiting.

Before you knew it, we were at it again, re-living Saturday night in a far more erotic atmosphere. The sun was still high and bright as were our passions for one another. But when we awoke, it was blazing orange, streaming through the windows and barely showing itself above the horizon.

Over the next few days, Linda took me to every acre of this gorgeous coastline to show it off as if this was her private estate. Back in Paris, she described Cap-d'Ail as a spiritual paradise. Now I knew what she meant. After all she had been through, this was now her life sanctuary, a place to heal from all the wounds inflicted upon her back in California.

One evening, we were taking in the view again from her jacuzzi. After reminiscing about our youth, she rose, dried herself with a towel and slipped past the sliding door into her kitchen. Minutes later she returned with an open bottle of wine and a manila folder. She handed me a glass while resuming her place in the percolating water and left the folder on a deck table next to her.

The aqua color sea was turning a darker shade while calming itself steadily in the backdrop of a setting sun. Before long, that sun surrendered its brilliance to artificial illumination springing up among the few homes scattered around us. We had been exchanging stories about our high school days back in the states, hoping to relive them somehow on the other side of the world. But Linda made it a habit of catching me off-guard with her spontaneous mind. She was now at it again.

"Lee, are you happy with your life so far?"

"What?"

"Are you happy with life? Do you like what it's showing you? Any big regrets? That sort of thing."

"That sort of thing can get very scary. I know one thing, it's going by real fast. I never thought about getting old, much less leaving the earth at any moment to points unknown. Maybe in the end, we're all just food for maggots, but this I do know, we take our precious time here for granted. So much is wasted. I can't think of a better example than divorce and family courts."

"Okay, if you had one wish, like in the Wizard of Oz, what would you wish for?"

"That's easy, a hot woman in a hot tub, and voila, mission accomplished."

"No, I mean it, why did you accept my offer to come here?"

Although it's not what she intended, I was a bit offended by her question, not sure if it was another ambush or whimsical curiosity. She had been massaging my calves with her toes and was headed for the thighs when she asked it, so the last thing I needed was a kick to the groin.

"I accepted because you're intriguing, Lynn, not to mention sexy, but I think we have something in common, something that could lead to extraordinary reforms for so many victimized families. The divorce industry gets away with all its abuses by pitting moms and dads against one another..."

"Oh stop!" Linda cut in, "You really know how to kill a buzz. Get off the court crap and stay on course. I asked you a question. Now answer it before I pour my wine glass over your head."

"... but by showing our unity as a mom and dad behind a greater cause for children, we can help shut down that industry."

"Get ready, counselor, here comes the vineyard." She was serious after all. My face became drenched in red wine. "Now shed the legalese. We're in a jacuzzi at the Riviera for Pete's sake. I'm trying to find the real you." After she wiped my face with her towel, I finally obliged.

"Okay, I get a rise out of helping people, doing the unexpected, accomplishing something to benefit future generations..."

"Let me get a different rise out of you," she cut me off flatly. "Have you ever had a soulmate?"

I could now confirm where I thought Linda was going with all this. I lightened up and obliged. Still, she was making me uncomfortable since her right leg was now within striking distance.

"I thought I did, kinda, but it was way back when I was a senior in college. She was a cheerleader and ..."

"Please don't tell me I'm going to hear a blonde bimbo story..."

"Oh, so you *are* a feminazi!"

I braced myself for a castration but fortunately Linda had a mutual interest which kept me intact.

"I'm anything but that. Just answer the question, it's simple really. What do you like in a woman?"

"Well, she's gotta be delusional, obnoxious, and hopefully psychotic. And that's just for starters."

"Come on Lee. Humor me because you're certainly not pleasuring me."

"Fine," I sighed. "Until I was rudely interrupted, I was trying to explain that I met the girl of my dreams in college. Only years later did I realize that she may have been my soulmate. I was too young with too many unsatisfied goals at the time. Not a fan of divorce, I let her go and ended up lost in space, you might say."

"What do you mean by that? You never tried to get back with her?"

"We never even made love. We were definitely hooked on one another though. I never met a lady like that again, and I still think about her to this day."

"Wow. That is amazing. Can't imagine how that happens without sex. So where is she now?"

"No idea. Last anyone heard she got married and had kids right after graduation."

"What about your wife, your fiancées?"

"What about them? Most people never find a true soulmate. That doesn't mean they can't fall in love. We're talking about two very different concepts here."

"Well then why did you marry?" Linda asked, straightening herself out on the opposite side of the tub. She shut off the water jets to better hear my response, one that was not expected. I was actually paying attention to her ordeal as she had been detailing it to me in recent days.

"The same reason you did, to have children."

"So she is a good mother then."

"I never really said she was not. But I don't care how much a 'custodial parent' puts on a show, when the other parent is alienated for evil reasons, it's a mortal sin to the children. Maybe these court warriors feel accomplished in all their exploits, but someday you gotta face your maker and be made to explain why you put your selfish interests over theirs. When they grow up, you can't fix a crooked tree. It's probably too late, and you can't turn back the clock of time."

Despite Linda's commitment to stay on course, she had already made the segue back to our ordeals.

"Yeah, but some parents are absentees, abusers and sickos. There's got to be a justice system which protects those little ones from serious harm."

"Oh come on, Linda, if you mean the current system, any mom or dad could end up an abuser. I've heard all kinds of false charges made between parents, as a lawyer on the inside and victim on the out. The irony of it all, there is no utopian parent to compare to. Each of us has a unique definition that could make all others unfit. That's how the system perpetuates itself. It simply keeps moving the finish line with a parenting figure that it never defines and the societal changes it incorporates."

"Wow I guess that explains why my lawyer kept billing me without alerting me to such realities. Isn't that a violation of ethics?"

"Yeah it is, a lawyer should have you informed on the vital aspects of litigation. Vague standards are at the top of any list. But this would mean a huge blow to fees and revenues. Now you're getting a reality check on my world."

I was eager to finish my earlier point. "But Lynn, I'm not talking about the actual ten percent or so that have no business being parents. I'm talking about the vast majority who simply can't get along with one another. That's no reason to exploit them for money and alienate them from their offspring. It's legalized kidnapping for profit."

I thought our side-track was over, but to keep me in play, Linda kept pushing my buttons. "Well, we gotta move on somehow, right? Why should the children have their stability disrupted just 'cause mom and dad don't get along?"

"Pahleeeza, Linda! You're making the stay-at-home mommy case here. Moving on? Try moving to the 21st Century. And stability, that's your back-up argument? Seriously? The state is always disrupting child stability regardless of divorce. At the earliest tender age of four or five, they do it for compulsory education. They bus them, place them with substitute parents called teachers, and upset their lives almost as extreme as birth itself."

"You mean to tell me shared parenting can't work as well?" I added. "If the state is going to remove children to enrich these predators, it should at least compensate them like eminent domain proceedings. Instead, it makes the victims pay for the kidnapping through fees and support."

"Well, what about step-parents?"

"What about step-parents? It's got nothing to do with them. They might even have children of their own. In my case, a childless man I was never introduced to was trying to make my daughters his. At least that's what my ex was trying to get him to do. He inherited wealth from his own parents, and she wanted a piece of it over my dead body. That wasn't going to happen no matter how corrupt the judges got. I already knew about those who were sent to prison for taking bribes, and I wasn't about to take any chances with my girls. Now how were they supposed to understand any of this?"

"I don't know, Lee, it sounds like you might've been a little jealous."

"Sure, if you like drama. But the reality is I'm jealous only for my precious daughters. You see that's the problem with this system. A guy can't get a fair shake no matter what he does. When he's pushed by these discriminatory laws to the outside looking in, people like you accuse him of jealousy. Worse yet, they accuse him of being a deadbeat, an absentee for protesting his degrading status as a non-custodial parent."

Reaching for my i-phone, I retrieved various photos of women I had dated since my divorce. If a photo tells a thousand words, this would be all the proof I needed. "Here, take a look at these photos. Now tell me I'm jealous."

As she studied a few, I went on, "The divorce industry today is one which manufactures one product and one product only. It's called conflict, no different than casinos that sell chance. There's very little that is genuinely productive. Lawyers go off with your money hiring pricey investigators and so-called child experts to tear down the other parent. In my court papers, I likened it to the Roman Coliseum. Boy did that piss them off." I chuckled mildly before returning to my proof.

"Look at these other ones from my photo library. With so many wonderful experiences with my girls, I have yet to hear anything positive about me in these courts. Sure, a lot of it is retaliation, but humor me at least. You risk losing that almighty custody award if you say good things about the other parent. And what kind of psycho brainwashes their children to hate that parent?"

"In the end, no matter what we do as dads, it's never good enough," I complained further. "There's never enough money to satisfy the scorned parent who thrives on the adversarial court process. It's a lucrative one for outsiders and the last thing that children need in their formative years."

"You must have seen it all as a lawyer."

"Sure did. I recall one incident where a mother was chasing her ex across the court lobby yelling out questions like, what's our kid's favorite subject, the names of all his teachers, and the last time he had a cold. She was obviously drawing from the custody playbook without regard to the tactics her lawyer committed to secrecy. She was freaking out with no regard for anything but her control dynamics. Now how was a breadwinner focused on a future for that boy supposed to know all the caregiver details. But that's the standard for custody decisions and the prejudice against a fit dad."

"Alright you're getting all fired up. Let's get back to this soulmate thing. Describe her for me."

"I really can't."

"Oh, come on counselor, again it's a simple question really, out with it. This isn't a bar exam." Linda loved getting deep with me, but once she got us there, she had this uncanny habit of deflating our discourse with anal diversions.

"Okay, here goes. My soulmate is a woman and a lady secure in either role. She may not realize her potential, but that's where a partner lifts the boundaries placed upon her and opens up a world she never knew existed. It's not an isolated event but a never-ending process fueled by true love."

"Oh my, you are deep. That was really sweet. I see what you mean by hopeless romantic. Please continue counselor. I'm loving this."

It was obvious that Linda and I were still striving for that ultimate partner in life, and she wanted to get my take, sending me that trademark smile for good measure. I think she did it just to make me uncomfortable at times.

"But if destiny is to make her your soulmate, she must do the same for you. We don't have to have the same interests. All I ask is that we live life to its fullest, together to the end. We take care of one another and don't run off when the going gets tough."

"You see, I'm also not the kind of guy who can be caged. It explains why I'm fighting these debtor prisons. Government is monitoring us in an anal way, like when a woman can't trust her man because she got cheated on. That never happened to us, but don't you think, subliminally anyway, that many moms use the custody award to control that which they could not during a relationship?"

"Huh, interesting. I guess I never thought of that. I'm sure it happens more than we like to admit. Well, does your theory change when cheating does happen?"

"That really shouldn't make a difference when it comes to the kids. Come on, you know what I mean. I'm just not the kind of guy who can put up with the control thing non-stop. And you can't presume me guilty because of your own past. My last fiancée was like that. She caught her ex cheating in the act. It devastated her and then she took it out on me. I never cheated on anyone. Even with all her lies during our custody war, my ex-wife never accused me of that. Both of them ended up suffocating me in the end."

"Well you're running out of time Romeo, you ever going to find her?"

"Maybe not, but it's not for a lack of trying. In the meantime, back in my single life now, I think of her as if she's in my arms and living forever in my mind. A figment of my imagination, granted, but I never want to let her go, because if I do, it's like we'll never take up where we left off, in the afterlife I mean. I know it all sounds crazy, but there's your answer from a mortality standpoint."

"That doesn't sound crazy at all, Lee, it's a dreamy ending to a great love story. How did you come up with something so awesome?"

"Well I had some inspiration from an old friend, Walt Scott, who once said: *True love's the gift which God has given to man alone beneath the heaven.* What about you? Equal treatment here. Where's your soulmate?"

"Still looking, just like you."

"Yeah, but just like me, you also got married."

"Yes I did, but I was pushed by my biological clock, ticking away as fast as that Grand Prix down the road. I can confess now that I was never in love with him. Still, I like to think if it hadn't been for these custody laws, we might've stayed friends."

"Sounds complicated."

"You'd think so, but this was a very possessive man. A different kind than you experienced. Sometimes that's attractive to a woman by the way, it can make you feel real special. Why do you think those mafia guys had those hot women? It sure wasn't because of their looks."

She reached for her folder and handed me a few photos of her own. It was evident that she had been keeping them handy for the bombshell she was about to drop on me.

"Look at this, Lee, it was taken by my investigator. There's my ex-husband with Jamaican drug dealers flying all over the place while his lawyers were filing for custody just to drive me crazy."

"Are you trying to say he's still doing that? Is he after you for some reason you're not telling me?"

"The blunt answer is yes, but we'll get to that some other day. Like

I said, I could use your help with international law. He knows nothing about this villa, at least as far as I can tell."

Before I could follow up with an assortment of questions, Linda got up, reached again for a towel and then headed for her bedroom. "You are coming, aren't you?"

"Sure, in a minute. You got me riled up right now. I need a Budweiser, maybe a six-pack."

"Alright, just don't fall off the deck."

This could be considered my first real disappointment with Linda. My risk-taking may have reached its ledge. I suppose anything's possible in the early phase of a relationship, but I felt betrayed by her latent disclosure regarding a volatile husband, potentially lethal and irredeemably possessive. Was I being used? Did she entice me here to become her legal and personal bodyguard?

Abruptly my sex drive took a coffee break. I needed to wake up to a reality that could escalate my risks here in Europe. I remained on the deck longer than expected. After an hour or so, sure that Linda was fast asleep from our long day of touring, I began surveying the sky for our Milky Way. I discovered it here for the first time. Our spectacular home showed itself off like no other place.

The sky was clear again. Every day I was here, there had been sun in abundance and no rain. Other than some stray cat that startled me at one point, the perimeter was quiet. I continued to study the constellations when, suddenly, I was alarmed by car doors opening and emergency lights radiating from the front of the villa. I threw myself over the deck rails and down the slope toward the sea. If this was Interpol or even local police, I was not about to become an inmate in a foreign prison.

I hunkered down behind a bush to monitor developments. After a few tense moments, I heard the car doors shut. The lights cut out, and the vehicle, with whatever was surrounding its brief visit, was gone. Then the area was filled with nothing but silence for a long time afterward, but I stayed put. They could not have come here for either of us because that would have taken much longer, and there was no indication of any lights or activity inside the villa.

I don't know how long I may have occupied my makeshift foxhole waiting for a safe return but eventually my mind started wandering to another place and time, far more pleasant ones when measured against my current state of affairs. Suddenly I was a kid again hiding behind bushes in the back yard of Wesley Miga's home. It was one of our Tom Sawyer sequels, and the bushes here smelled a lot like those did even if the events were decades apart.

While Wes was out cold at midnight with his bedroom window still open, I was attempting to signal my arrival for a clandestine road trip on our new ten-speed bicycles. In those days, any minor riding around past a nine o'clock unwritten curfew would be apprehended by police and escorted home for some serious discipline. But we were risk-takers and our sixth grade classmates were always anxious to hear our war stories the next morning. So far, we had not gotten caught.

I was at it well past midnight chucking pebbles toward that window. Unfortunately, crouched in hiding, I was reduced to a poor marksman. I must have hit the wrong window. I knew that when Wesley's dad, ever the home protector, came flying out the back door with a flashlight and tire iron. He gave no indication that he had been studying my location from his dark kitchen window.

Off I went across neighboring yards actually gaining on my pursuer. I would have escaped to freedom but as I rounded a side yard for the open road, the lawn turned into driveway. The blacktop was only inches above the level of that lawn but enough to trip me at high speed onto the surface.

Before I knew it, Wesley's dad had me in custody with blood pouring out of multiple parts of my body. Escorted to a home now lit up, Wesley's mom began tending to my wounds while the neighborhood watch commander endeavored to seal an indictment.

When the interrogation of their son and his accomplice was complete, our stories agreed. It became clear to these parents that we were simply being boys out for an adventure. What was equally clear, however, is that I could not be exposed for this prank to my own father.

Everyone knew that the punishment on my end would be harsh. So after much pleading and cooling of fatherly emotions, better judgment prevailed. Mr. Miga drove me home and watched me climb safely and undetected into my bedroom window. I never told anyone of this sequel. You're reading about it for the first time.

Strange as it may seem, I cracked a smile thinking back to that event. I also pondered how both our dads might be laughing together at this very moment from the high heavens. I rose from my foolish position, retraced my route back to the villa and concluded that a French patrol must have ventured up the wrong access road. Then I took shelter in my assigned sleeping quarters.

CHAPTER 8

AMBER ALERT

The smell of eggs, bacon and home fries was permeating the bedroom even with the door shut and the window cracked open. I wasn't sure whether it was that or the seagulls that woke me from a deep sleep. I was a poor cook and relied on diners to keep me alive back home. So this was a welcome break from that routine as was my new alarm clock.

"All rise, counsellor, this ain't a food court I got going. If you wanna eat, get your butt down here."

Linda would've made a great judge. Unfortunately, politicians have the inside track on those jobs. After visiting the bathroom, I joined Linda in her kitchen. She was gradually indoctrinating me to her legal matters, and we routinely discussed our ordeals over breakfast. I didn't mind despite that scare the night before. We had become lovers joined by fate. I wanted to help her where I could and she seemed mutual about it. Today she felt comfortable enough to introduce me to her son.

"Hey Lee, take a look at these photos from last year back in California." She beamed with love and pride as she placed them next to my plate. They featured a cute little boy in a pre-school setting. Linda carefully described the background behind each one. I hadn't seen this side of her since I got here. Her eyes were glowing with a sincere smile beyond the trademark version.

"Wow! He's so cute. I like the one with the football jersey." I moved that photo closer for a better inspection. "What's his name?"

"Gerry," she replied still passing me more photos. I envied her condition. It was so much more humane than mine, all those days wondering where my daughters were, how they might have been doing at school, whether they were even safe. In most other respects, we were kindred spirits, victims of wolves in black robes and suits.

"When I look at photos like these," she continued, "with all of what we've been talking about, it motivates me more to challenge this custody system. We shouldn't be fighting over a prize like this. What kind of life is it for me and my boy?"

"That's what I've been trying to tell you all along. Where is he now?"

"That's what I've been wanting to tell you all along. It's why I need your help."

"Go on…"

"Gerry is with a friend in Paris."

"That place where you had our cab drop you off?"

"Yeah, there. I'm concealing his whereabouts from my ex-husband until I can get protection here in France along with a stay-away order against him."

"But I thought you said it was all tied up in the courts of California."

"It is. My ex-husband is not the real father, and we weren't married at the time Gerry was born. The real father walked away from his responsibilities. Actually, he wanted an abortion which I could never do. It goes against all my beliefs."

"We agreed to leave him off the birth certificate," she explained further. "Then when I got married two years later, my husband became his dad. At least that's the way we treated it. Everything was good until the physical abuse started. I did not want my son raised in that environment."

"So you brought him overseas because I'm guessing a California judge is granting access rights."

"Exactly, but it gets more complicated because now the lawyers want to know all about the real father and why he was kept off the birth certificate. They're calling what we did a fraud. If the real dad is brought in, he might try to assert his rights now that he's matured with a good job. It's a real mess that's got me very stressed and worried."

"You should be. I think your bigger problem is going to be criminal kidnapping across borders."

"Not if I can get a French court to grant my petition. Gerry's not been here that long, and I got several lawyers working on it. So far, it's been tangled up in jurisdiction issues."

"Wow, that is a real mess. Why didn't you tell me this sooner?"

"We've only been together less than two weeks. How could I? Still, you could be a life saver here."

"I don't know, Lynn, I'd like to help but my daughters were effectively kidnapped due to corruption within the justice system. It's hard for me to sympathize with you on this."

"Even if my ex is abusive and the real father an absentee?"

"No, I get that, but it's a slippery slope. These are also highly abused custody tactics. You sure you're not crying domestic violence just because you don't like what he's saying, maybe an argument that got out of hand, your ear drums the only real contact he made? I should know about this game. First, they force you out of a child's life, then they label you an abuser or absentee."

"And I get that too, especially with all of what you told me. But I can show you the proof."

"Save that for the people you really need to convince. In my case, it was not about justice or the best interests of my daughters. It was about a gold-digging mom and a millionaire boyfriend she wanted to replace me with."

"I may never get my true daughters back," I lamented. "They've been cloned to be their mother contrary to the laws of nature. Plus, I can't do this court thing anymore. They've made their sick point in a killer way. My health is now at stake. I'm no good to my girls dead by any court."

I reached for a sip of coffee and continued. "I'm not doing the world any good either with a crusade so divided among the victims it'll never see daylight. So I gotta try something new, something extraordinary to get overdue reform. One case at a time like you're asking me here is not going to make a dent in this crusade. Other victims are pushed to their limits with violence and even murder-suicide. [38] But that's not me. Contrary to this honey badger reputation, I abhor violence."

Linda sunk her head in disappointment, but I pressed on with my emotions rising.

"And somewhere along the way of this crusade, I expect to be compensated for my heavy losses, like anyone who loses a child to a criminal or drunk driver. That's how they got it all backward. Instead, the wrongdoers are rewarded with revenues and support entitlements under that federal funding law. I lost precious time to where I don't even recognize my girls anymore. I'm..."

"Well, hey, you..."

"No, hear me out Lynn. Back home on the way to the airport, I passed by the school where my daughters were, unable to check up on them because the ex and family court would be all over it. They treat caring 'non-custodian' parents like neighborhood drug traffickers or child predators. Actually, they treat the real criminals much better. It

---

[38] <u>Pearce v Longo</u>, 766 F. Supp. 2d 367 (NDNY 2011)

got me recalling a time when all this got started, when I came to our first school orientation for both girls."

"While mom was focused on my elder daughter in a first-grade session in one part of the school library, I snuck over to the other side where my younger one was seated on the floor with other tikes, legs folded and glued to the librarian doing a kindergarten presentation. I did a little test to see if I should engage in the custody war which I knew their mom was going to trigger, the sick conflict I had seen time and again as a lawyer."

"As I got closer to the front, Cassandra took note of my presence and screamed out, 'Daddy, daddy, there's my daddy.' She pointed excitedly in my direction with such a glee that my test was passed with flying colors. Now how could I walk away from that? The rest is history. But today the system has done its dirty work so horrifically that neither daughter bothers to contact me in any fashion. And that same system can come up with nothing sane to justify any of this."

"That's such a sad story," Linda declared, reaching for a Kleenex. "I guess I never really knew how dads struggled with all this until I became a victim myself."

"Family court litigants are like lemmings when they run to these courts for attention," I elaborated. "How we gonna achieve reform if we don't call this what it is? It's our duty not only as parents, but as citizens, to test oppressive laws."

"Ya think? I've been doing that to the tune of more than a hundred thousand dollars. But what's the use?"

"Parent revolution is the use. We'd still have separated races in our schools if a black father, and I stress *father*, hadn't brought his little girl to a white school in the early fifties. A unanimous Supreme Court opinion resulted that changed America. [39] You could learn a lot from me, Lynn."

"Alright I'm all ears."

"After years with no contact, I was finally able to get a court order to have my girls over for the holidays. To my shock they ignored me, and much more. They managed to erase every sweet memory of our time together for over a decade. The alienation was that profound. Last we were together, it was all hugs and kisses as I watched them head for mom's car down my driveway. With nothing else occurring since then, other than public criticisms, I was now some kind of villain."

"Did you try reaching out to them, explaining what happened?"

"Of course I did, but first off, a novice judge named Dan King kept placing obstacles in my path. Visibly offended by my exposure of his errors, he abused his public trust by imposing conditions for child access, some that were conflicting to a point of contempt by ambush. He made it too risky to comply. Within months of my testimony against him before this corruption commission, I lost all contact with my girls. There was no evidence to support this vindictive alienation agenda with the ex. Hell, my parenting time had been doubled only a year earlier by King's predecessor, a veteran judge I might add, after another costly trial. No one I appealed to gave a rat's ass."

"Wow, they really did target you."

"Second, I was under a court order not to talk about litigation which is all but impossible after the court took control of our lives. The judge even gave them a childless old lawyer with a hatred expressed against his own dad at my custody trial. It's in a 2009 closing statement. I got the transcript to prove it. Now how does that make him a competent child lawyer?"

---

[39] <u>Brown v Board of Education</u>, 347 US 483 (1954); <u>Brown v Board of Education</u>, 349 US 294 (1955)("Brown II")

"Third, I did what I could to offset that alienation, for example, playing videos of our wedding and early years as a family to offset the venom their mother had injected into their minds. Nothing I did or said worked especially since I had only a few hours with them over two holidays at that point. When we returned to court on the issue, the ex tried to make my efforts out to be 'bizarre,' as she put it, while demanding jail on support arrears. It was a real twilight zone, let me tell you."

"More like a funny farm."

"Well said, Linda, I like that depiction. You know, when I was their age, I got physically beaten on a regular basis but never erased my dad. I cherished our good times and loved him to the day he died. But what's going on today is something which civilization has never seen before."

"They order all sorts of hideous evaluations, Lynn, to enrich other court predators while the truly sick world impacting our children gets away with murder. I mean, who's evaluating the sick minds of the evaluators? Who are these people to play God? It's pure evil, utterly satanic. We're seeing an end to parenthood itself."

I pondered my next remark but went for it anyway. "At my dad's funeral, it's the only time I can recall that I broke down publicly. It was while I gave his eulogy. You gotta wonder if these custodial offspring even know what a eulogy is today. A judge has to be something short of a Nazi to accomplish this parent alienation thing. It's inhumane beyond belief. This is our so-called civilized court system? I hadn't done a thing wrong to my girls. We had the times of our lives together."

For a moment, I began reliving those times: "During separation, before the predators came along, I was the first to take them to Disney World, the ocean, skiing, hiking, you name it. I built them a giant playground. We even had this routine every Christmas where I would recreate the Polar Express movie and act it out like Tom Hanks at my home. It was so special, we would…"

I cut myself off knowing that my emotions would pour out if I continued on this train of thought. Linda reached over to console me. After a deep breath or two and looking away toward the sunrise streaming through the kitchen window, I recomposed myself and returned to our discussion.

"These were their most vulnerable years of child development without any mishap or report from anybody. One time I caught Kristen by the arm just as she was about to dart in front of a speeding car trying to get to a playground from a side street. I was there for my daughters when all the predators were taking courses on how to enrich themselves as child rearing experts."

"If a father fails to return a child on time, takes his own children an extra day or even a half hour, he gets an amber alert like a common criminal, an all-points bulletin, at the very least a contempt citation followed by a childish scolding from some bombastic judge who could really give a damn. He wasn't there when they were born. What did he do to raise them? Why even bother running to court for permission. It's no wonder so many people are choosing violence over this foolishness."

None of this was new to Linda. She was familiar with such experiences but still not ready to accept her litigation strategy as an overt kidnapping even after my reality sermon. To prove the kidnapping scam in my case, I got up from the table, left for my bedroom and returned with an e-mail confirmation notice, an exhibit at one of my more recent hearings. I showed it to her and continued.

"See this? The so-called mother failed to report a relocation of my daughters' residence to this millionaire's home. These girls are not for sale Lynn. He had all sorts of background issues. The old home address was retained for more than eight months on the court record while she was hauling me in for support, living in a free home, and collecting undisclosed rental income. Eight months! She never got so much as a lecture for faking notice to get around our custody order."

"But wouldn't you know the change of residence from the child exchanges?"

"Those exchanges ended a year earlier, when the speech retaliation made them impossible. As I just explained, it was contempt by ambush with all the growing and conflicting conditions. When we *were* making exchanges, it was at a neutral location by her request. Regardless of that, she was under court order to notify me. Even convicts get a right to know where their children are living."

"Yeah, I remember reading about a case like that."

"The girls went along because, I'm sure, despite laws against it, mom was showing them decisions making me out to be *delusional* about custody requests and a *dead beat dad*. Those were her words and how she answered my petitions for parenting time, sworn statements filled with lies and grammar errors, from a high school teacher no less. Over time, with judicial approval, it had her actually believing in her own lies, or at least acting that way."

Again, I took deep breath, shook my head in disgust and took another sip of coffee which was now cold. I left my chair, shuffling aimlessly across the room to the parlor area to note that the morning talk show was focused on childrearing dysfunctions and drug addictions. I watched for a while and then resumed my place at the breakfast table. Linda was silent, finally glued to my reality.

"This was the most basic information about my children's living arrangements. There are parents imprisoned for life who get court ordered visits with their children. In my case nothing was done, not even phone calls were enforced. Now you can't tell me something else wasn't going on here."

"I can't imagine going years without hearing from my son, Lee."

"I can cite one case after another where moms addicted to heroin were aggressively treated and reunited with their children, another who left her infant on the floor in human waste while passed out on drugs. Child protection had to come after the child and the mother did some jail time after that. Yet her lawyer got her reunited shortly afterward."

"He's the same lawyer assigned to my daughters," I added, "claiming to be protecting them. I've never even been accused of any crime, never been on prescriptive medication, okay except maybe penicillin at a young age. And I've hardly seen my daughters in nearly seven years! It's an injustice of monstrous proportion. You'll never convince a rational person otherwise."

Edgy now with all the coffee in my bloodstream, I got out of my chair again and moved around a bit while continuing our discourse. Then I walked her through my court papers, explaining further, "Look right here, where it says *gmai.com* on this e-mail claiming notice of relocation? See anything that jumps out at you? I proved a fraud not only on me but the court as well. It was pathetically obvious by the lack of an address character 'l' in her so-called notice."

"Yeah, it's obvious alright, no computer expert needed to figure that one out."

"My twelve year old could figure it out at the time. And still mom testified under oath that the transmission was successful. Now how does a sane judge, let alone a fair judge, accept this as fact? But he let it go after she blamed it on an old computer even though her sworn affidavit beforehand made no mention of that. No big deal. A white male was the victim. And you're going to tell me this judge is not promoting a kidnapping to avenge my criticisms? Talk about an Amber Alert!"

"Or maybe he got bought off," Linda suggested. "See I don't trust these judges any more than you do. I read about this Brooklyn judge,

Gerald Garson. I remember him because he's got the same first name as my boy. The lawyer for a dad offered him $9,000 to fix a custody case. The mom somehow managed to get the FBI involved and the judge was convicted and sent to prison."

"No need to cite one-sided. Look up Judge Thomas Spargo. He too was caught trying to fix a divorce case in favor of a mom. It involved a lawyer dad, like me, no less. Imagine all the judges that never get caught? It's all in the unwritten play book. What's the difference between abusing judicial office for a bribe or for censorship? What are we supposed to do when our civil channels for recourse are shut off? Take matters into our own hands? That's kinda what you and I are doing."

"How do you figure?" Linda reacted, still defiant about her side. She had never been subject to a child support order and had no interest in obtaining one. She only wanted full control of her child.

"Remember what I told you about *Bast v Rossoff*, [40] a mom and dad, both lawyers earning roughly the same amount of income." Linda recalled our discourse on it but still came across disinterested. "They derived their own support arrangement. Still, they were required to name a custodial parent under that federal support and funding law. State revenues were never mentioned in the decision."

Linda was not paying close attention, and I could tell she had no idea what I was trying to educate her to. She patronized me with interruptions but only with an empathy needed to get me back on her side. Our talk went well into the afternoon.

"It's all about the money, and I can back that up. During my reform efforts, I came across two dads and a mom who together spent over ten million dollars in lawyer fees alone. Now how much sophistication does it take to make a 'best interests of the child' argument? My ex-secretary

---

[40] <u>Bast v Rossoff</u>, 91 NY2d 723 (1998)

did that without a law degree or a license, ran her own fake divorce practice for years before they finally listened to me and arrested her. Look, right here, there's the news article."

I showed her an article with a Pretend Attorney headline and quotes from a county deputy who declared that he had never seen anything like it. "I packed the court room with her victims on the day she was committed to jail on $10,000 bail. She quickly got bailed out, probably with some of the money she stole from me. It occurred in another county and not mine where most of her crimes had been overlooked to that point in time. I contacted the court there earlier that day with the background information, unconventional maybe, but certainly justified. And it worked."

Suddenly ready to offer a thought, Linda asked, "Imagine all the unproductive jobs this custody industry creates, Lee? It really is a form of child abuse when you think about it. This is a giant bureaucracy punch drunk over money. Many of these forensic contractors contribute to judge campaigns. That's the quid-pro-quo. You don't need a G.E.D. to figure this one out."

Linda's delayed input was actually more profound than she may have realized. As I had experienced in my law practice, psychiatrists could offer addicting drugs or a temporary fix to the symptoms of a crisis, but a good lawyer with a conscience can remove the crisis itself by promoting settlement or mediation. In these courts, a profit motive makes such a cure all but impossible.

"Divorce and family court programs could be summed up as therapy for a broken system, Lynn. It's an adversarial framework which has no place in a forum involving innocent children. It clashes with cooperative parenting in contrast with a court truly acting in our children's best interests."

"Once in the system," I warned, "you're on Satan's docket, it's a downward spiral. If a mom or dad comes in angry with one another for whatever reason, that hatred can be magnified many times over by greedy lawyers. By the time they're done, you will hate the other parent like you never imagined, like you were trained in hell itself."

"Wow! I never heard it put that way, by a lawyer no less."

"As an old friend once said, *Revenge is the sweetest morsel to the mouth that was ever cooked in hell.* Think of it as the Confederate states in the day preserving race discrimination by treating the anger issues of slaves with anxiety medication. It's the same sort of anger here. The only difference is that the victims today have the means to afford the so-called professional services."

"We definitely live in an over-medicated society," Linda quickly added, "no doubt about it."

"They get you fighting over your own offspring, and if you love them enough, it's what you do naturally. They even make it sound heroic. Before you know it, they got you under constant scrutiny, escalating conditions, bankruptcy, jail, maybe even a mental institution. In the end, they blame it all on the parents. They can't make this gold mine work any other way."

"I see what you mean now." With prominent anger, she reiterated, "In less than a year, I was forced to spend over a hundred thousand dollars to protect my son and me from abuse. I'm not rich. I worked hard for that money, and my ex has a lot more of it to finish me off. They're literally killing me, Lee. So I'm all for reform. Can this system get any more broken than it is now?"

CHAPTER 9

GENDER SKIRMISH

We continued to war with the custody system, our adversaries and each other from time to time trying to find a solution to a problem that was well beyond our capacities. We chuckled here and there when trying a more light-hearted approach to our objectives. But this was hardly a subject for entertainment. That's when a solution arose that we could tackle very easily.

"Hey, Lee, let's go over to this yacht basin nearby," Linda suggested with excitement. "There's a great restaurant with a patio overlooking the docks. We can loosen up together and finish this conversation with fruity cocktails. Imagine what else we could do? It's too nice to be inside."

"Sounds good. I love yachts especially since I owned one once. That's long gone too."

We ended up seated at a quaint café known as Le Fabuleux Destin. Our table overlooked a marina filled with various sized boats and small yachts. We had a light meal with ice cream for desert. Then we sat back under a blazing afternoon sun. Linda sipped on a Pina Colada while I nursed a bottle of Heineken with no Budweiser on the drink menu.

We watched casually as tourists and boat enthusiasts passed us by. At one point, she asked me about her fate if she lost her case here in France. I answered as best as I could without scaring her. I made a prediction that we would both end up in the same jail cell together. We continued our discourse focused on her dilemma until it degenerated into a dispute that was near and dear to me.

She opened the door to a gender dispute with a remark that was sexist in nature, a sort of hit-and-run slur she thought I would simply shrug off like most dads do. But I was not about to let her off the hook. She referred to the biological father of her child as a "dead beat dad." It wasn't the first time she used that phrase. And as far as I was concerned, it would be the last time she used it in my presence. I confronted her, and she asked me why I was being so sensitive.

"Sensitive? It's a sexist slur! Try going around the streets spouting off racial and ethnic slurs and see how long you last. You'll wish you had domestic violence. You keep using the male pronoun every time you bring up the subject of child support. Why is it that child support is always *his* child support and not *her* child support in everyday talk, like we dads not only owe it but own it too?"

"Hey, that's …"

"No," I cut her off angrily, "you're acting like that Arizona governor, Ducey, whatever his name is. I call him Douchey, a spineless politician playing to the women vote. He published child support wanted posters for dads only. Dead beat moms got a free pass. You'd think he would be focused more on the real criminals bringing drugs to the same children across the Mexican border."

"What if you see your son on one of those posters some day? There's certainly no reform on the horizon, so maybe you better brace yourself for that stigma. You give me this lecture about a man's duty to support his children while ignoring this new millionaire father. Haven't you been listening to anything I've been saying these past few days, the parental alienation, all the reports about it?"

"Of course, but…"

"So it applies to dads too, the vast majority of victims fed up with this gender biased system. They're walking away from their children because of all the abuse and coming unglued in violent ways. More and more, experts are concluding that this fatherless society of ours is the reason for so many other costly problems, the lack of respect for laws, morals and authority." [41]

"Hey, don't forget all of what I've been saying either. I'm with you on that. I see it every day in neighborhoods even around here. I think this women's rights thing has gone off the deep end. It's now hurting moms like me. You're definitely on the right track there."

"Good, now that we're back on track, let's stay there. I spent years fighting back enemies on all sides just to have a relationship with my daughters. They simply turned that around by claiming this was my way of avoiding support. Truth is, they just wanted to keep collecting that money."

"And it was tax-free to the ex at your expense," Linda chimed in. "That's easy money with the state giving her legal services and adding the cost to your support bill. That's also your message!"

"Linda, in the true America, or in any free world country for that matter, we agree to disagree. You don't have to accept any public message, but when they go out of their way to crucify the person behind that message, it becomes tyranny or censorship, no different than any other vile regime."

---

[41] Professor Stephen Baskerville, *Is There Really a Fatherhood Crisis?*, Independence Review, Vol. VIII, n. 4, Spring 2004, pp485-486 ("What many are led to believe is a social problem may in reality be an exercise of power by the state.")

"And I'm sure having to defend against so many attacks, it hurt your ability to pay child support."

"Of course, but shouldn't it be the other way around? Shouldn't I be paid for the government fraud on the public, the seizure of my children through oppressive court orders? But they never gave a damn. Even my enemies wondered how I was supposed to pay so-called child support after they took my licenses, vehicles and what was left of my savings that I needed to start a new career. And how do you do that with all the reputation damage? Yeah, they were very calculating."

"You really think they planned it to come out that way?"

"Let's put it this way. They're certainly not stupid, at least not as they pretend to be when it serves their agenda. The harm was fully predictable. My ex received over $45,000 in tax-free support one year despite my unemployment and was never required to account for expenditures. I was actually paying a millionaire to play dad without my consent. You said it right, Lynn, a real funny farm."

"Okay I'll buy that after what I've been through. Nothing surprises me anymore. They were just screwing with you, Lee. It's so obvious."

"I called it judicial waterboarding in my filings with the Supreme Court. Every time some troll accuses me of being a dead beat, I shoot back that I'm a modern day Susan B. Anthony. She refused to pay her fine for the crime of voting just like I refused to pay support for the crime of fathering. Ironically the courtroom named after her is the same one where my law license was suspended."

"They simply never gave any credence to my stand against human rights violations. Then when they tried to put the anti-woman label on me for promoting those rights in family court, I answered that I once represented the former president of the National Organization for Women. But my cause was much more. I took this stand against a *pay-to-parent* system that alienated my children."

"I get all that, but…"

"No I really don't think you do…"

With offense taken, Linda reloaded and took aim. No longer patronizing, she took the offensive. "But aren't you really hurting your daughters in the end by taking on this crusade for people who don't seem to care? I mean they're going to need college funds before you know it. I know you love them no matter what they do. They seem like smart girls, so eventually they'll figure it out and return to you on their own. But child support is still important."

Linda really knew how to push my buttons, I could see that, but was she seriously that naïve?

"Next time we do this discrimination thing, Linda, I'm going to record it on my phone, so I don't have to keep repeating myself. Hey, I'm hurt every day, every moment my girls don't call me. They're well into their teens now, so brainwashed by their gold-digging mom they see no problem with that. So I'm supposed to throw more money at this evil system? Over time, they can always get child support, as they call it, but I can never get time back with daddy's little girls."

"By the way, how did you manage to get that pedophile judge off your custody case before anyone knew about his sexual abuse? I mean those private sessions in chambers are standard procedure."

"I know. Call it a daddy's premonition. And fate certainly had its play to make. That's why I filed something unexpected, a motion to have him disqualified altogether from my case for another reason, political espionage exposed by his chief family court clerk. If he could direct court staff to spy on judge candidates, he could do the same to me as a public figure."

"Political espionage? In family court? What the heck are you talking about Leon?"

"Hey those aren't my words," I answered defensively. "They came from a federal court where Judge Hedges and his boss, District Chief James Tormey, were sued for retaliation by that court clerk. She opposed their spy directives on a judge candidate of the opposite political party, the same one I belonged to. I held public office and was an endorsed candidate for senate on that party line. And they knew it. She recovered $600,000 against them. Look it up, *Morin v Tormey*." [42]

"Wow, that's politics interfering with the administration of justice!"

"Damn straight. And Tormey still retained his leadership post in Syracuse. He's the one who assigns judges like the ones in my case. He also handles certain lawyer and judge complaints as district overseer. Anyway, during my arguments, lawyers for my children and their mom chastised me, declaring that Tormey's co-defendant, Hedges, had a reputation beyond reproach, at least until he resigned after admitting to sexual abuse of his own five-year old, handicapped niece."

"That is a shocking irony. But nothing surprises me these days."

"Easy for you to say, Linda, but that's what happens when you take religion, authority and proper parenting figures out of our children's lives, exactly what this profit system does. In a televised debate with me, one lawyer simply trivialized it all by declaring that the system was *imperfect*. [43] Are you kidding me? Imperfect? Try horrific."

There was a long pause as she sunk her head. She knew that I had hardly seen my girls in years without any finding of unfitness and a diary filled with wonderful father-daughter activities. Having talked so incessantly on the subject, she was also enlightened to my tortured crusade to preserve father and mother figures in separated family units, values that made our society possible.

Still, she remained obstinate in her own crusade against domestic

---

[42] 626 F. 3d 40 (2nd Cir. 2010)

[43] Sarah Blazonis, YNN News Syracuse, New York (March, 2010) www.leonkoziol.com

violence. Fair employment practices were all-important in the twenty-first century but in Linda's world, working moms were still returning to homes in Pleasant Valley circa 1950s. In the day, judges called it the *tender years doctrine* which is still alive. She wanted it both ways, however unjust the outcome. To deflect from her illogic, she abruptly asked me to give her my option to child custody. I responded swiftly.

"It's ironic that a divorce lawyer asked me the same question as a co-host on a radio talk show recently. He must've assumed I had no good answer because a good lawyer never asks an open-ended question without some idea of what to expect, at least during any cross-examination. So I'll give you what I gave him. I brought out that option under the general heading of shared parenting, because that was a term that was fairly known by most listeners."

"But," I continued, "my version of it had the legal profession out of the *child business* as one judge put it in my presence. If there was to be a custody order, it would not be mandated by any federal funding law. Instead, it would be the exception to that mandate only if one parent was truly absentee, truly abusive or the parents could truly not get along. All tactics to cause lucrative proceedings would be banned with all offending judges and lawyers held strictly accountable. None of this was unattainable, but I could see it offended the co-hosting divorce lawyer."

That settled, once and for all, our gender skirmish. Then, from our vantage point facing the sea, we looked away toward a setting sun. It was dropping fast, taking the azure sky with it. The scene reminded me of the ones back home on the lake at the end of a fun-filled day with my girls. But here, at this moment, it was having a surreal impact not only on the landscape all around but also our mutual conscience as caring parents.

As I joined her gaze across the Mediterranean, my thoughts turned to that giant ball of flames, the only confirmed source for our very existence. I wondered how it managed over such an immense span of time, evolution and human generations to bring Linda and I to this point in our trivial dispute. That sun remains our most crucial and reliable event between dusk and dawn, the mother of all mothers. A solar flare could end our world tomorrow. We take it for granted so routinely.

Maybe the ancient worshippers had it right all along. Maybe our world governments should be less concerned about removing petty dictators and more about removing a piece of our planet to outer space. We need a truly permanent home while that sun continues to burn out, for our children of the future, like those domed city space crafts on that Boston album cover. There's a bigger human picture here. Instead of arguing, maybe Linda and I could make our tiny contribution to that end.

If history has any lesson, the racial and women's equality movements would never have succeeded without the moral partnerships formed with white male civil rights lawyers. But intellectual Linda had conveniently forgotten her history in a quest for today's gratification. She was preaching poor me, the mom, victim of abuse with crocodile tears. Yet when it came to my suffering, she pulled a Rip Van Winkle, like she just awoke from a prior century.

Somehow dads can handle it better, isn't that what she was really saying? We're tougher. We belong on foreign battlefields spilling our guts or risking our lives on the streets and in burning buildings. A violent soldier, dedicated cop or hard-hitting lawyer has no place in the parenting world according to so many family judges who privately practice this sort of discrimination. It's no wonder suicides are escalating in the male dominated, life-saving business.

So if we read Linda's hidden message correctly, it's perfectly legal to abuse fathers simply because we were born differently, as long as you don't talk about it publicly. And should anyone try such shenanigans, we'll pound him with lies and corruption. Welcome to my world, a dad deprived of his offspring due to a biological fact that I was born with an extra appendix for all our conversations were worth so far. Did she understand anything I walked her through regarding these custody laws?

Custody remains an abused classification that is archaic and inflammatory. It should be a status of last resort when one or both parents are found by *clear and convincing* evidence to be seriously abusive, neglectful or to have abandoned a child altogether. In countless cases, custody wars have become a parent termination process which requires greater due process protections.[44] Instead, shared parenting is the exception when it's even acknowledged.

Like Judge Duggan emphasized in the *Webster* case, custody and visitation have outlived their usefulness. To preserve this lucrative framework, dads remain default victims, weekend warriors without genuine rights. There are no men left in the divorce industry. Its "architects of justice" sold their manhood to the almighty dollar long ago. At least that's the way it seemed to me after so many years of practice. Fortunately Linda was on to another subject that we could both agree upon.

"Lee, you mentioned this federal judge whose job it was to safeguard our rights in state courts. Why did you go after him too?"

"You mean Gary Sharpe. It's serious Linda, because you have a son who may face one like this someday. If you love him, get ready to feel his pain because I've seen this kind across the country. Moms then find themselves impotent to help their loved ones. You're right, federal judges are the primary guardians of our Constitution, they're supposed to promote federal protections, but too many are promoting their egos

---

[44] <u>Santosky v Kramer</u>, 455 US 745 (1982)

instead, like Gary Sharp who invents a human gene to make decisions. I'm not making it up."

"Yeah right," she responded incredulously.

"A federal judge actually declared on the record in open court that he found a human gene which the scientific community would not discover in another fifty years to make decisions. Suppose I showed up as a dad in a custody trial claiming I had discovered a gene which causes judges to take bribes or lie in their decisions. I would've been sent to jail or a psych ward right away."

"Wait a minute, back up," Linda cut in with a sudden awakening to my point. "Did this really happen in a federal court? I thought that's where the elite judges were."

"So they say, but they're appointed for life and not elected. Think what you will but it happened. It was so demented for our system of justice that a federal appeals court in Manhattan removed Judge Gary Sharpe from that particular case and said his decision was a disgrace to the judiciary."

"Imagine if a judge can just make up a gene to decide if whites or blacks should have different jail terms, custody orders or working conditions? We would have no need for juries or lawyers in that event. But I won't get into it all, you can look that case up too, called *United States v Cossey*." [45]

"Hey, I'm not saying that judges are anything like Gary Sharpe. There are great ones, very hard working and properly dedicated, lawyers too. I'm friends with lots of them. That's also why I won't tell you about a judge who showed up drunk for a night court arraignment on a DUI case. He was reported and required to attend AA sessions. None of it made the news."

"And when it does, rest assured politics could be the cause behind it.

[45] 632 F. 3d 82 (2nd Cir. 2011)

Take, for example, that recent case about a mother who filed a domestic violence charge? She never even showed up in court for her own trial. The judge, a woman by the way, held her in contempt and hit her with a three day jail term. That was a small penalty when you compare it to six months for child support contempt."

"Now how do you operate a court system if filers can do a hit-n-run like that? Women's groups went ballistic anyway. They protested that judge for being so harsh and it got all kinds of media coverage. Never mind this kind of harshness is going on all the time with guy victims or that allegations are not proof. The charge alone was career damaging with huge defense costs. But the accused here just didn't matter. Neither did his due process rights. That judge was actually reprimanded for her conduct.[46] We need more bad moms in jail to equal the playing field here."

Suddenly Linda's eyes welled up as she cupped her face with her palms. A flood of pent-up emotion was cutting loose. It caught me completely off-guard. My best guess was that Linda might now be facing a jail term of her own on a more serious charge of kidnapping. I did not expect this reaction.

To my dismay, she surrendered her chair and fell into my lap, curled up like a baby. I tucked her in and protected her in every way I could from inquisitive minds along the marina docks. My gorilla looks in their direction got them scurrying for their boats.

She was trembling uncontrollably now. Linda was a tough woman, but I had seen monster guys, football types, in my civil rights cases who broke down the same way. I watched incredulously one time when a

---

[46] Rene Stutzman, *Seminole County Judge reprimanded by Florida Supreme Court*, orlandosentinel.com, August

30, 2016

prison guard cried openly on the witness stand before a jury in federal court.

The judge even recessed so he could recover. As my client later explained, his psychiatrist predicted this when he was finally able to spill his guts. The real cure came when the case was settled right after that. We recovered $300,000, but a member of the jury informed us later that we would have been awarded all $6 million we were asking for had we not settled.

In Linda's case, I sensed that the system had ganged up on her like it had me. She was pressed in too many directions with far too many burdens for a single mom to bear. I hugged her and caressed her until her emotions settled. Then I kissed her on the head and said nothing. Before long, to my amazement, she was snoozing like an infant.

That was fine by me. Linda had not slept properly in a long time. During my stay at her villa, she would get up at two and three hour intervals, never a solid repose from all her languishing fears and anxieties. Over the years at the lead of this grass roots parenting movement, I had come across many situations like this, war veterans, minorities, homeless, the list goes on. The victims could not be counted. I even took calls in the airports and on my personal time to handle crises.

I don't know how many suicides or homicides I prevented, but I do know this: the hope I generated during those phone chats, on-line exchanges and public appearances may have saved hundreds of lives. They could not be recounted here but as I continued to give human shelter for Linda in such an unexpected way, I thought about a dad in Suffolk County, Long Island.

He was an unemployed parent deprived access to an alienated child, a loving dad left with only a decrepit van to his name converted into a makeshift home. He would find a way to visit me whenever I came to Manhattan.

On one occasion, he drew a blueprint of sorts on a napkin at an Irish pub near Times Square. It was done to convince me that he really did live in a van for three years because of this Title IV-D corruption. He too seemed to have that law well memorized.

He was later arrested and jailed, not for back child support but for a theft of utility services after plugging his van generator into an outdoor receptacle of a retail establishment. He had been patronizing the same business for essentials and the managers let it go for a long time.

Seeking help from like-minded victims, he attended reform rallies when he could. Suddenly after one of them, an anonymous complaint sent him to jail. Then, while in his cell, they got him for his back support causing an outrage among sympathizers who patronized the same business.

He was promptly released but his van had been impounded, leaving him to his survival skills on the streets. I hadn't heard from him since last autumn and that worried me because such victims could easily be a cousin or close friend. Last I knew he was braving the winter elements.

I don't know how long Linda had been out cold in my embrace. I cuddled with her as best I could in my difficult position. As I looked down on her from time to time, she was peaceful as a child, protected from all possible harm.

I continued to survey the environs. Sea gulls occasionally caught my eye. The clanging of sail rigging and banter of tourists around us tapered off. Beyond that, all was sublime. The sun was achieving an amber hue as the day progressed. Then, suddenly, Linda emerged from her slumber.

"Oh wow, where am I?" she asked, rubbing her moist eyelids.

"You're in the land of Oz, where'd you think you were, on the

Riviera or something?" I smiled down at her as she reciprocated with a mound of embarrassment.

"So does that mean you're the lion ready to take on my custody judge, the wizard of court corruption?" She responded playfully with a punch to my shoulder and squeeze of my bicep.

"Yeah, I guess, it won't be the first one I exposed on my website, but if I've proven anything it's that I'm no coward. Looking back, sometimes I wish I was. No one came to my rescue after I gave up everything for this righteous cause. Where was Toto when I needed him?"

CHAPTER 10

SHARK ATTACK

Linda was an early riser, and that meant rumblings outside my bedroom door before sunrise. She could typically be found in the breakfast room making love to her laptop by the time I got up. But on this particular morning she was nowhere to be found. I searched her entire villa on the expectation we would be making plans to address her kidnapping issues which were quickly coming to a head.

I called out her name from time to time on the back deck but gave up when I could see that her beach bag was gone from its usual location. More disconcerting, there was no breakfast plate awaiting me on the kitchen counter with the routine microwave instructions whenever she stepped out.

She had been accustomed to an early swim at the seashore to avoid tourists. They were not locals as she considered herself. A bit of a loner, Linda got great satisfaction wading in the shallows at La Mala, a short stretch of sand at the west base of the cape. For my part, it was becoming burdensome arranging for transportation beyond Linda's neighborhood. Even the nearest coffee shop was miles away.

The easy solution was a small motorcycle leased from a vendor who delivered it to Linda's villa. It arrived for the first time the night before after I ordered it during her snooze at the café. As soon as Linda spied the intruder in her driveway, she threw it a dirty look, as if Hell's Angels had just parachuted in. Hey, it was no Harley, so there was no reason for her to defame the little tike.

"What's this now? You gonna go off on that noise-maker to meet the guys at Stars 'N' Bars?"

"Oh come on, Linda, that's not fair. I've been enough of a burden on you driving me everywhere I need to go. This is the answer. Heck, I can't even go to church on Sundays without getting you behind your steering wheel and then waiting in the parking lot for your return one hour later."

"Hey, I'll say it again. You impressed me with that church routine. It was no burden. But as far as I'm concerned, it's one big hypocrisy. You won't find me inside. I get nothing out of it."

"And I'll say it again. I don't go there to get something out of it. That's just a typical reaction of a me-first society. I go there to thank God for the blessings he's given me: my life, my health, two beautiful children, and the great host I found here. I'm no holy roller, it's just that I can't take the arrogance of humans as the know-it-alls of creation."

I pointed into the sky from her deck that night before and emphasized, "How can you look out at the infinite stars each night and not see God in the mix, this concept of light years, our inner biology and not conclude that there's a higher power to worship? Like you say about this picturesque cape, it's a spiritual thing."

I added "great host" to my list of reasons to offset any offense that may have been taken. But it was increasingly evident that a schism was developing between us. Her use of gender slurs to describe child support debtors was answered by terms that depicted her controlling nature.

She would often supply the gratuitous addendum of assuring me that she was only joking, but her tone and body language screamed otherwise. Whether she picked up on it or not, I used her full first name whenever our interactions got tense. And the motorbike was a vile intruder.

For me it was a godsend. She must have looked over the bike again in the early hours today and reacted. I was ready to do just that until a note taped to her refrigerator caught my eye. From it I learned that Linda would not be home for dinner due to a sudden meeting arranged in Paris with her soon-to-be, ex-husband. Hopefully, she would convene at a public place with a friend as a supporting witness.

Either way, I felt used and now abandoned. She could have discussed this with me face-to-face. Something just didn't add up. It was time to shed my concern for her. With no information on Linda's whereabouts right then, I struck out for the coastline. Beyond the irregular streets, past the manicured grounds, far away from the lawn sprinklers of her hillside neighborhood, I became liberated of all the stress she was adding to my ordeal.

Within minutes I came upon freedom, the pounding of waves along the highway, leaning from side to side with each curve in my lane, palm trees flying by, smiling up at the warm sun on my face, inhaling the invigorating aroma of tropical flora, it was the essence of life.

It was also long overdue. For years I had heard every imaginable nightmare in America's divorce industry, one horrific war story after another, the vast majority of which brought me no income while my utilities were being shut off. I once charged hundreds of dollars hourly, and now I was being treated like some free legal aid service. My predatory adversaries had done their job well.

It got me often to a breaking point, one that had to be tempered from time to time, and this was one of those times. I knew there were many lost souls out there. Much as I wanted to, I could not save them all. That was government's job, our third branch, which had caused this epidemic in the first place without any concern for their manufactured victims.

When I was practicing, it got to where I could tolerate the corruption no longer. How many times I had to observe parents tortured by lawyers profiting from a custody framework that was so dysfunctional, children were actually being ordered to spy on their moms and dads. What did these freak predators, so many that were childless, know about our children?

How often I had to endure judges and lawyers at the end of a "business" day with a partially concluded session citing vacation priorities to extend a continuance. They did this audaciously after making clowns of their clients who had to listen to all their exotic plans made possible by needless, inflated fees. Stressed-out parents hoping to get their nightmares concluded as quickly as possible were forced to set their hearing schedules in conformity with these lawyer get-aways.

These were not courts of law, they were shark tanks. Wherever family issues could be concocted, there you'd see the feeding frenzy. In all my years on both sides of this tank I could never understand how so many intelligent parents could plunge headlong into these unholy waters only to fall victim over and over again. Even my reform allies continued to pay into this system.

They were the mammals of Seal Island waddling into the treacherous waters off South Africa, endeavoring to cross False Bay only to be scarfed up by great whites. But these court predators were nothing like the impressive sharks, they were more like the mangy buzzards of a dried-up swamp plucking away at a carcass known as divorce.

Such were the ugly thoughts cast to the wind behind me as I passed gas along with it while racing to a destiny I could never have imagined when passing my bar exam so many years ago. And I suppose that's what made this whole ordeal so exciting in a sick sort of way. I could not envision where the next turn on my fateful journey might take me. Only months ago I was being

threatened with contempt in snow country. Today I was riding aimlessly in a tropical paradise.

My little motorbike, responding so dutifully to every directive, was immensely therapeutic. For now, only sex or exercise could exceed this feeling. So I decided to name my newfound buddy, Linda Lovelace. I'm not really sure why that came to mind at this pleasurable moment. I only recalled her as the first famous porn star and a fitting response for the woman on the hill.

I stopped for breakfast at a roadside restaurant and was not pleased with the ambiance of the place. It was not like the ones back in the states where a waitress greeted you and included a local paper with your coffee, real coffee, not expresso in a shot glass. The waitress here had a shapely figure and character bold enough to insult me with witty jokes. But she politely reserved them for her regular customers. They appeared to be the common type, my kind of people.

Unfortunately, these days, such diners were becoming obsolete, replaced by chain restaurants obsessed with the bottom line as if their profits were eternal. Keypads were converting patrons into products to reduce overhead costs. I couldn't get out of those places fast enough.

Many wait staff today required parent-like guidance, perhaps due to a vast shortage suffered during childhood. We see the symptoms of career moms, divorce and family courts everywhere. Children are being raised by strangers, day care, educators, even friends, all parent substitutes. The New World Order was falling into place faster than parents could keep pace.

Indeed, since taking on this cause, I had seen society through a different lens. It was therefore a pleasure to see that ever reliable paper notepad show up in the left palm of my waitress when she returned, a vestige of our traditional past, the European version of the *Guest Check* headed for some restaurant museum.

I ordered my usual eggs over light with home fries and Italian toast. I then grabbed a hold of a British house paper for some news from back home. Donald Trump was front page again, taking aim at another politician and television reporter. It's as if our entire world had obtained a reason to get up each morning. He brought a lot of revenues to those media outlets he called fake news.

Inside, there was a feature regarding another black man shot dead by a white police officer. It seemed that such atrocities were becoming a regular occurrence even after the Walter Scott murder. The white traffic cop there finally accepted responsibility and was sent to federal prison.

Nevertheless, as I studied the article, I thought back to all the law enforcement I had represented, retaining a high regard for their daily risks. I had saved careers, both black and white officers, from false claims. When the facts came out, the conclusion was often at odds with the verdicts in the press, and it is rarely mentioned that a black cop was also charged in the Walter Scott case.

I then turned to voice messages and e-mails on my i-phone, surfed for social media news and concluded that all was good. One of the benefits of a defamed and underemployed state is that stressed out clients don't call you, at least not a fraction who did when my time was in demand.

Oh, poverty parts good company, as my friend Walter Scott would say.

Another friend, John Kalil Jr., was the only one who checked in on me daily, and that had not occurred yet. He would be the only one to suspect if I was alive or dead. After downing a coffee refill and leaving a nice tip, I was off again, riding Linda Lovelace under a gorgeous sky.

If there's one obvious negative about a two-wheel mode of transportation, it's that your risk of injury or death is elevated many times. I learned that lesson the hard way years earlier on the Mexican island of Cozumel.

I had just come off a cruise ship at one of our ports-of-call to discover that all the newer motorbikes had already been leased, a price you pay when you're opposite of Linda, a late riser. That left me with a cheap, likely defective motor scooter to explore the island.

It was all going too well as I enjoyed the view off the rugged road on the unpopulated east side of the island. Like here, the surf was pounding the shoreline as I made my way to the next tiki bar in the middle of nowhere. Suddenly my front wheel caught a sizeable pothole sending the scooter into psycho mode. I knew I was going to hit the blacktop, no shirt or helmet, but to stay reasonably intact from a bodily standpoint, I had to ride this horse out as long as I could.

I hit the blazing hot pavement like a stone skipping off a pond, my skin peeling off in so many locations that I looked like a human tomato when I finally came to. The scooter was shot and laying somewhere in a sand dune whereas I was dazed and lucky to be alive.

There I stood on a rough, narrow road in the middle of nowhere with no one around to figure out the extent of my injuries. Eventually a small tour bus made its way toward me from the opposite direction. The driver and passengers simply stared in horror as they passed me by. Behind them was a Mexican road patrol.

The driver exited first and looked me over. His partner immediately got to his dispatch with the urgent message that I needed an ambulance and emergency room as soon as possible. Now when a Mexican cop makes a call like that, you know it's serious.

I quickly advised him that I would not be submitting to any emergency service, definitely no hospital. I was alright I insisted and with a good cleaning at some rest room, I would be ready to re-board my cruise ship. Both were aghast at my statements but compromised with a transport to an EMS at their nearest firehouse.

I eventually made it back to my ship cabin hobbling up the gangway like a modern day mummy. I thought my left leg was forever maimed, but I never did visit a doctor. To my amazement, I fully recovered in a matter of weeks with only a few scars as proof of my death defying event. It was one which made me extra cautious on the Riviera. In Cozumel, the incident report contained the first known record of a recommended wall to keep crazy gringos out of Mexico.

There were so many sites to visit along the coast that I had to forget about that scooter mishap. I stuck mainly to the natural attractions. Soon enough the sun was setting across the sea when I found myself in the city of Nice. I obtained refuge in a restaurant and bar known as Wayne's Pub, a neighborhood tavern in old town with an Irish ambiance.

After a fine steak dinner, I settled down with a couple of cold ones to reminisce over a challenging but satisfying day. I had long forgotten Linda's rude abandonment of me when this day got started. I was young and free again, and for the moment anyway, my nightmares back home were in remission.

A stray magazine on the bar caught my attention with a feature regarding the terrorist attack that occurred not far from where I was seated. On July 14, 2016, a cargo truck plowed into a crowd of pedestrians celebrating Bastille Day along Promenade des Anglais killing at least eighty-four. To think I could have been one of them. I wondered if my ex would be celebrating then.

A trio of sax, piano and guitar players had just opened live entertainment when five women assumed the seats on either side of me. One was particularly attractive. Bubbly and full of life, she wore pink shorts, a loose white blouse and sandals. It was hard not to distinguish her from the rest of this group. A few guys in the vicinity suddenly lost interest in a soccer game on the screens above the liquor shelves.

For the record, I'm not a player. My standard tactic for wooing the opposite sex remains a rather lame one. I would simply eavesdrop to see if an opening was allowed my way. A dirty look was usually enough to get me running for the exit. If the coast was otherwise clear, I would pounce like a rabbit. This was one such time. I politely offered to relocate.

"No, no, stay put," replied the attention-getter. "We just came in from Monte Carlo and what a bunch of bozos we ditched there. At least you got teeth and a physique," she laughed. "Hopefully you'll tolerate us because we're more of a crazy but fun-loving bunch."

I smiled and said nothing in return. She looked me over and continued. "Are you a tourist or local? My guess is the latter. The name's Terri by the way." She reached over to shake my hand, very business-like, as if we had just concluded a settlement conference. I felt compelled to rise before I obliged. To my delight, her touch was warm and inviting.

"I'm Lee, and the answer is neither. I'm here on…"

"Hey, whatever, come on. This song that just got started, you never hear it anymore, and I love it. Time to get down."

Before I could resist, she whisked me away by hand onto a makeshift dance floor, moving and swaying to Billy Joel's, *Scenes from an Italian Restaurant.* As I got close, her features invited further attention, blonde hair and baby blue eyes, a slender body that advertised itself with every curve and with each dance move.

She was no candidate for a dance contest, but hey, who am I to judge? On the next song, I saw an opportunity to walk her through a few moves and she went for it. Her girlfriends began humoring themselves over the scene, but in the process they attracted their own attention.

The capture of Terri's gang was made complete when my competitors escorted them onto our floor one by one.

We all danced and laughed, giggled and hollered, giving those around us something to talk about. A few others got onto the nearby tables to show off some Aussie maneuvers. As for our group, an eviction was pretty much court ordered by everyone else in the place through facial expressions alone. A couple of the guys had sufficiently offended them with their John Travolta routines. We got a round of drinks and then surrendered incognito to a rear table after the kitchen closed.

Group conversation followed. The girls were spending a few weeks with their sorority alumnus who lived in Monaco, the one named Terri who got this all started. They were entertaining us with stories about guys they had ditched during their nights out, having opened with one such incident occurring only hours earlier at a sports bar in Monte Carlo. My new comrades were evidently delusional enough to believe that it could not happen again on the same night.

"Man, you girls sure are a lot of fun," declared a guy named Victor with a smile that lacked sincerity.

"Yeah, Kate and Karen had us busting a gut about Budapest beauty and the creeps of Calcutta," added an assertive fellow named Max, still proud of his Travolta routines. "Your romance stories are coming across like a real comedy."

"And we're just in time to make better ones for you," offered a third suitor with a pronounced southern drawl. The rest of us did not really know what to make of his comment, but he introduced himself as Ted. "I'm from Nashville where we never sleep. Dance music everywhere at every hour," he beamed. "Where are all the hot spots?"

"Mostly here and in Monte Carlo, Ted," replied a guy named Carl. He was here on business with a home base in Kansas City. "I've been exploring all week and haven't found much outside of those places except beachside restaurants unless you stick to the resorts."

He threw a smile in Terri's direction and kept his eyes fixed seductively on her shoulders. I could see she was struggling to end the attention but failing now in her seated position across from him. After a visit to the ladies' room, she returned strangely quiet. Her girlfriends must have assumed that this Carl guy was too fast for her or that he was simply not up to their social standards. I wasn't sure what to think, but for the moment I was enjoying the drama.

A fourth candidate did not introduce himself. He simply remained enamored by the company and dialogue as if high on something or maybe he just hadn't seen a woman since the past century. Either way, it didn't matter. He was buying all the drinks and we were buying all the bull being marketed among this newest cast of characters on our collective journey of life.

"Okay, we'll get to more of our stories but first, a toast: Here's to the bottle-in-front-of-me and not the frontal lobotomy."

Mary-Beth, a boisterous stout woman who could easily have passed for the sorority enforcer was intoxicating herself to a state that might well lead to the surgery just referenced. Between quips and outbursts, the girls took turns describing events of the past two weeks. The guys did their best to reciprocate. For reasons I still could not figure out, Terri continued to distance herself from the dialogue.

I pretended not to notice, but she kept alternating glances toward the bar and entrance as if anticipating another arrival. Her shifting demeanor was suspicious, more like the dread of a jealous husband stalking the area. For me that would be a rescue the way this migraine encounter was shaping up with these strange dudes.

Fortunately, Karen saved us from whatever catastrophe might be awaiting. "He's here," she announced quietly from Terri's left side with a sense of urgency. "Let's ditch these losers so he doesn't think we're with them." Seated on her other side, I could overhear the peculiar exchange.

"You sure? Mare's a bit toasted, and I don't trust that guy who keeps staring at her."

"He's staring at you, idiot. We can all see that. Besides, they're big girls. They can join us later at the hotel. There's gotta be something going on at the lounge. Come on, they're playing these guys like we were at the other bar. I already told Kate our exit strategy, and she's good with it."

The private exchange apparently led Terri to conclude that a better opportunity would not emerge tonight because she whispered something in Karen's ear while reaching again for my hand under the table. Then she rose and rushed for the door with me in tow as if a blow-out sale had just been advertised. Once outside, she let go and raced down the street.

"Where you going?" I yelled in my confused state on the walkway. "And what's going on?"

"That's for you to find out, Lee, if you're man enough anyway. I'm getting my car. Follow me!"

For all I knew Terri was using me. Maybe there was some jealous guy she was setting me up to confront for ego purposes. I had seen that adolescent routine many times back home. Or maybe the girls were genuinely being stalked by their earlier suitors.

Whatever the explanation, this was no idle challenge. I couldn't just ignore it especially with the way she concluded with that sexy giggle. I didn't bother to think this out. Time was of the essence, so I quickly revved up Linda Lovelace and gave chase.

At first, she was nowhere in sight. Then, from a side street, a shiny red Porsche pulled out in front of me and sped down the city streets.

Terri's scream out the window was as recognizable as the rest of her when she spotted me on the bike.

It turned into a chase scene as the streets gave way to open highway, a winding route familiar to me only because of my earlier drive here. And that was during the daytime. Now my cycle skills on every sharp curve or blind descent would be tested to their limits. Suddenly I felt like I was back in Mexico as the midnight rider.

This was obviously not just any man-challenge. I was keeping pace with a woman suddenly turned wild who was testing how far I would risk my life to make her mine. I thought about my fugitive predicament but by now there was no turning back. I was far too committed.

There was still a lurking thought that she was making a permanent getaway. But with every mile I conquered, it was looking more like an adventure of a lifetime whatever the outcome. This Terri woman was acting like Danica Patrick of the Grand Prix in Monaco which was now just up the highway. She shot through a tunnel headed toward Monte Carlo.

We never made it that far. Instead, Terri led me down a winding road toward the seashore. I rounded a bend with a drop-off on my right. The Porsche had come to a standstill in a lookout spot. Before I could pull in behind, its tail lights kicked off and she vanished.

I quickly took note of an access trail to the beach which she obviously intended to have me follow. On the chance our stay might be long, I hid the rental under a distinctive olive tree to mark its location. Cicadas and crickets kept guard.

I looked around and could find her nowhere. So I hiked down the access trail and struck out for the open beach. A strange moon was lighting up every little depression and mound in the coarse sand. The sea was mildly turbulent with silver reflections skipping off its surface. A foreigner in an exotic land, I asked myself what I was doing here.

Presently I stumbled upon a large rock near the shoreline where Terri's clothes had been thrown into a pile on top. Her pink shorts, bra and panties were all there like road signage for a porn shop. It was erotically stimulating to say the least. I looked up and down the beach, back toward the dunes and finally out across the sea. She was nowhere to be found.

I called out her name, getting more bewildered as this adventure progressed, now with a concern that Terri might have become the victim of a shark attack. I had seen the documentaries, but this situation was very real and new to me. The only sound I could discern was that of rippling waves at my feet and a vehicle on the precipitous road behind me slowly navigating its way eastward. Then all was curiously silent.

Suddenly I was drawn to a head piercing the surface of the dark water about fifty yards in front of me followed by a blood curdling scream. The first thing that came to mind was something I only imagined from the movies, being swallowed whole by a great white while trying to save a swimmer from one of its mates. I limited those nightmarish rescues to women and children.

Hey, I'm all for male bonding at a sports bar, but shark fights are not a recognized sporting event. Sorry guys, you're on your own in these situations especially if you're like those dudes back at Wayne's. Where were they when you truly needed them? I could have had each one distracting the shark while I rescued this damsel in distress.

Fortunately it was all a prank. Gasping for air, Terri managed to laugh loudly while treading water. "I got you Lee," she cried out. "And don't say I didn't. You really thought I was that college girl in Jaws. I always wanted to do this to someone. I just wish I could've gotten a better look at your face when it finally happened."

She continued to humor herself over the event, ever proud of her achievement on this warm Riviera night. Now I realized what that moon was all about, to put a spotlight on my dumbfounded appearance. I wasn't sure if I was angered or pleasantly relieved.

"You are the quintessential bastard!" I yelled back. "All this time you were putting me at risk to carry out a sick prank? It wasn't funny Terri." There was no immediate response as I thought about it further. "You mean Karen even helped you set me up? I was ready to pry you loose from the fangs of a hungry shark. And how was I supposed to do that anyway?"

"With all your manliness and chivalry," she hollered in return before slipping beneath the surface. I kept my eyes peeled, spotting her farther out a few moments later.

"With that scare, you won't find me anywhere near you now."

"Oh come now, little boy, don't be a baby," she teased. "And stop with that 'quintessential' bullshit. What are you, some kind of lawyer?"

"Actually, yes, but I like to keep it private so that I can have more friends."

"Well then what are you standing there for? Get out of those clothes and come on in. If you want friends, I got one for you right here, and it's really wet."

"And have a giant fish take a chunk out of my leg? No way! I don't care how wet you are, I like my body parts."

"I'm only interested in one part, Lee, and trust me, it ain't your leg." She continued to laugh and tease me with mild insults. "Come on college boy, don't be afraid. Your cheerleader's out here and she's got something for you. Bet you can't guess what it is..."

After disappearing and surfacing again, she gave additional assurances of my safety. "Besides, there's no way any shark is going to bother us now. If you're a lawyer, you get professional courtesy."

"Very funny. Come on, let's cuddle up on the dunes instead, where it's safe. A half hour since we got here and it's been fairly quiet. We got the whole beach to ourselves. Here I can give you all kinds of professional courtesy."

I must admit looking back on this sensual exchange, I still get aroused by it. We continued to taunt, joke and flirt with one another but neither of us was surrendering our positions. Terri persisted in her demands for a skinny dip while I stubbornly adhered to a work-out on the sand. Breathing heavily at times, she simply side-stroked right and left among the glistening waves, tempting me incessantly while managing to keep our dialogue intact.

"You know, Karen wasn't really a part of this. It was all my idea."

"Then how do you explain your body language, this guy she said who just shows up? I heard you girls talking, you know. And why did you rush me out the door?"

"Aw, that's so sweet, Lee, you're actually jealous."

It was a statement which paralyzed me. I guess I never expected to be taken so accurately summed up. Could she be right? I couldn't help pondering the possibilities. From lover to soulmate in less than a day, it was all happening so fast. In a rare moment, I was speechless.

"To put you at ease, though, the stalker part was no joke," she explained. "It's true. I moved to Monaco last year from Dallas to get over an abusive ex-boyfriend."

"Is every ex-guy an abuser these days? I'm sick of hearing it, and what's he doing here anyway?"

"Hey, I'm actually serious. Some of my girlfriends are witnesses. I even got the scars to prove it. Karen thought she spotted him back at Stars 'N' Bars near my home. He's rich and powerful, thinks he owns me."

"I guess that explains the new Porsche."

"Karen thinks he got wind of their trip," she answered, deflecting from my conclusion. "He might be looking for me here. I wasn't about to take chances. You just happened to be in the right place at the right time, and it's getting better by the minute at this beach. You're so sexy standing there and looking stupid. Come on in!"

"Why would your ex-boyfriend be stalking you now?" I resisted, somewhat disappointed with the lurking thought that this ex of hers might come charging onto the beach with a hit squad.

"I'd rather not say. I don't know you well enough. But it helps that you're a lawyer. So you coming in or not? Do I gotta fake another shark attack? How would you ever handle a real one if you're acting like you are now?"

"That's easy, I'd call a lifeguard, same thing every other red-blooded guy would do today. Ya think I wanna expose myself to an arrest when a woman is being attacked? That's a VAWA violation back home. And then I get eaten alive on top of it all. Hey I'm all about chivalry, but those feminists have destroyed it with these crazy laws."

"What the hell are you talking about? Now I know why you keep that lawyer thing to yourself. It's really turning me off. Last call, Lee, shut up and man up. I can't believe there's a hot naked woman in the water out here and a fully clothed guy standing there on the beach talking about some violence law…"

I can't tell you what she said after that because I had been hatching my own prank. In an effort to keep our communications alive, Terri had gradually floated her way close enough to become my prey. If I could swim across lakes, this feat would be a walk in the park. Her measured distance and location were about as good as it was going to get.

I had kicked off my sneakers, slid partially into the water, and when she last dipped below the surface, I began breast-stroking swiftly along the sea floor in her direction. I reached blindly for my target and caught hold of one of her ankles. Before she could utter another word, down she went into the dark depths of the Mediterranean with a shriek that could be heard in North Africa. We surfaced soon enough and laughed together at my revenge.

Next thing we knew, all was quiet again. We treaded water for a while before moving into the shallows, our eyes fixated on one another as if this would be our final life embrace. The talk of sharks had us both stimulated in a very erotic way, hearts pounding only inches apart, lungs keeping pace, our naked bodies bursting with desire in the backdrop of a moonlit sea extending to earth's horizon.

Nothing more was said. We merged, exploded and were swallowed whole in our ecstasy.

CHAPTER 11

EARTH'S CHILD

We were having dinner perched atop a cliffside terrace on the Greek island of Santorini when my predicament back home came to a head. That terrace belonged to a restaurant in Oia known as Ambrosia. It boasted a spectacular view of the island's caldera, a volcanic depression filled with seawater and surrounded by five islands that shaped its half-moon, center bay.

Santorini is the most phenomenal paradise I have ever visited. Located among the Cyclades, it was ground zero for the largest known volcanic eruption 3,500 years ago. It blew out the center of the former island leaving the surviving five sides intact. The resulting tsunami devastated the island of Crete nearly a hundred miles away. A sun-bleached community here contrasted with aqua color waters far below to create vistas that would take your breath away.

It was also a great place to escape a child support warrant procured through corruption. That was my objective when Linda flew us here. Like her exotic hide-out, this would be mine. I did not question her absence from the villa on the day of my bike excursion, and she did not question my absence the following morning. Instead she sought to invigorate our relationship by considering an option if her landlord came calling or our fugitive conditions became real.

She was instantly enamored with my depictions of Santorini. I had first visited here fifteen years earlier on my honeymoon. And like Sacred Heart Basilica in Paris, the archeological site at Akrotiri was missed on our itinerary. We arrived just as the place was closing earlier than expected. It therefore ended up on my bucket list. Linda was far more curious intellectually than my ex-wife was, so it only made sense that she would finance a re-visit.

But only days after our arrival, I had gotten word that my adversaries back home might be pulling back. The support warrant which sent Linda into rescue mode had not been issued. Foreclosure on my home would be the method for payments as prescribed in a 2010 court order. At least that's the way it was explained on the phone. Dinner conversation was now focused on our future together.

It should never have come to this. That order was violated the same year by collection agents from the state tax department. As they rationalized their crimes, the state had acquired a "tax lien" on any support arrears referred to its collection centers. Pure gobbledygook, who was going to stop them? I tried in vain. Our government had succeeded in creating a tax on children.

In a growing number of states, there was nothing left to tax. New York, for example, had settled a lawsuit with the federal government over Medicaid fraud which required it to pay back $10 billion. That money had to come from somewhere and naïve parents were a perfect target. They could be relied upon to pay for the state's corruption. It became a pay-to-parent scandal.

For now, that meant that fugitive status was no longer a threat. Surprisingly, Linda did not share my relief, visibly disappointed instead.

She vigorously warned that this was a set-up, and given all the craziness of my ordeal, I privately feared that she was correct.

By the time I got the news, Linda had already prepared a final escape for us to Ireland. How could I tell her about Terri? How could I explain the opposite directions we were taking for our children? She was all about antiquated custody awards and I was ever committed to progressive shared parenting. A jalopy versus a spacecraft, how could we ever forge a lasting relationship?

Even if we could overcome our gender issues, my heart remained wherever my daughters were, and that meant it was an easy decision to make. I obtained return flight tickets the same day despite the continuing saga back home which could suddenly bring me back.

That's the way I eased the news to Linda, sensing her growing attachment; a tender, protective, motherly oversight that I considered rather sexy. But as far as I was concerned, our partnership never really materialized. Reluctantly she nodded her understanding but was determined to change my mind.

We stumbled upon this restaurant while browsing various boutiques along the narrow, winding cobblestone streets of this ancient town. Earlier in the day we had been out swimming in the bay on a private charter boat. It was off-season, but the otherwise cold water of the Aegean Sea was remedied by steaming lava mounds of a still active volcano at the center of that bay.

I remember visiting those barren mounds during my honeymoon. It resembled a Martian or lunar terrain. No matter where I stuck my hand into the lifeless surface, its subterranean heat registered profoundly on my hand. I could also remember diving from the rigging of a tour vessel that got me there. It bore the trappings of a pirate ship. The waters were as warm then as they were now.

A waiter approached with menus as I sipped tenuously from a coffee mug. The local water would assuredly upend my digestive system. The heated version of make-believe coffee would be less risky than the untreated cold glass variety. So I gulped it down and awaited my own microscopic eruption. Linda was similarly tenuous but anxious to get the most of our remaining time together. I was scheduled to fly out of Paris by the end of this week.

"Lee, I need to know what keeps you motivated?"

"Whataya mean?"

"Motivated, you know, how do you do it? I've only been at this about a year, you've been fighting the machine in New York for more than ten years. I'm already taking anxiety pills but you don't seem to be affected. Crazy, maybe, at times, but you're relentless in your mission."

"I guess you could say it's genetics, my family lineage, whatever it is that got us to survive centuries of evolution. You and I, for that matter all moms and dads, are the fittest of our species. Through natural selection, our ancestors made it possible for us to be at this romantic overlook."

"You really believe in that Darwin stuff?"

"Only because it makes sense, confirmed by the things I see every day. I'm glued to nature and it's kept me healthy despite all the chemicals we take into our lungs and stomachs. A nature hike clears out the impurities like nothing else. Only a couple hundred years ago, there were no factories, electricity or computers. Our parents' parents survived through physical exertion, loyalty, true father and mother figures, and the laws of nature as opposed to the law of profits."

"Okay, got you so far, but what can one person do about our collective destiny? I mean why not move to Ireland with me? You said it yourself, survival. This mission is killing you, and you already made it clear back at the villa that you'll never get your true daughters or your law license back. So why not open a practice in Ireland, start a new life? There's gotta be a law firm which could use your unique skills."

"Good point. Tempting as that is, there is also a spiritual force driving me. Government freaks are gradually destroying us, Lynn, whether they know it or not, and the vast majority of parents don't see it. So I've taken it upon myself to alert them to the blitzkrieg that's coming. It's not just any mission I'm on. This war on parents is very real. The children of today and generations to come, if they even get here, are relying on us to preserve the most ancient right of humanity."

"But it's gotta be taking a toll on you. You're no good to your children dead. You said that too."

"Well my ex might see it otherwise. But that's how the lucrative custody system works. No amount of hate-driven fees is enough. As far as my health, you may be right, but so far the good lord has spared me serious maladies. He also spared my life in many harrowing circumstances. There's gotta be a reason for that too. Hiding out in Ireland is not it. That much I know. You gotta minute, 'cause I'd like to tell you a few stories to back up this spiritual thing?"

"Sure, we got all evening. The moon is just starting to peek over the sea, and Akrotiri isn't until one o'clock tomorrow. I could sit here all night with this gorgeous scenery."

"One time on a hot afternoon at a place called Lake George in upstate New York, I was swimming around my boat. The future mother of my children was above me on the front deck with friends enjoying cocktails. She pretends to be such an angel in court but I drove her home drunk many times after our boat excursions. As you know, I only drink buds neutralized by physical activity in between. Our boat was big for a lake."

I pointed over to a small aft cabin motor yacht tied up at a dock in the distance. "See the one with the British flag over there, it looked like that."

"Geez, that is a good size. It had to cost you."

"It did. I christened it *Defense Rests*, but it's all gone now. The predators seized it through attrition. I couldn't afford to maintain it. My girls loved spending time on it. Anyway, my stereo was loud, everyone thought I was swimming around a small island as I usually did. But actually I was underwater wrestling with my anchor after the boat drifted toward others anchored nearby."

"Repositioning it manually was a lot easier than starting my twin engines and disrupting our guests. But a gust of wind hit the bow just as I was moving it. I was only in three feet of water but also knee deep in muck. Suddenly, the anchor line went taut around my thigh. There I was with ten tons of boat keeping me below the surface."

"No way! Meanwhile, everyone's just partying away, right?"

"That's right. I swam three miles across that lake the same year, and here I was drowning in a shallow bay. I was about ready to suck water into my lungs, end my life, and then..."

I hesitated, knowing that what was coming out next would not be accepted in the world as Linda knew it. "Then..., well, that's when something miraculous happened whether you believe it or not. I saw my future daughter pleading with me to come out of this. The vision of her matched the one at our last Christmas together four years ago."

"Oh man, you're giving me goose bumps Lee!"

"I still get 'em when telling this story. Suddenly I felt super-human, like that mother I heard about who managed to lift part of a car to save her baby. I pulled the anchor up with my last bit of energy with my face turning purple. I quickly removed all the muck on it, enabling me to free my legs with a lighter load. Then I got just enough distance to bring my mouth to the surface for a huge breath of air. That was sixteen years ago before we married. As you can see, I survived."

"I wonder if there's a family judge who can give us a ruling on your parenting skills at the time. Now I see what you mean by religion being destroyed in these custody courts. They would laugh at that story even though it made your girls possible, the ones they're profiting over."

The waiter returned, took our orders and politely disappeared. He was obviously more observant than the ones who barge into a conversation with all the rudeness of an ignorant bull. I liked waiters like this one. I continued with my stories.

"This cliff on the side of our table drops down over five hundred feet. When we got here, it reminded me of one back home that I'd also like to tell you about. Twelve years ago, I got a sudden urge to climb the high peaks of New York. Up to that point in my life, I had only climbed one with another forty-five left to conquer. It's as if a higher power was getting me in shape to survive the ordeal which was to come."

"I didn't even think they had mountains in New York. How high are they?"

"They're the alpine variety, those over four thousand feet where pines can grow and leave- bearing trees disappear. The highest one, Marcy, is over a mile high, but you gotta remember they're also lower to sea level. The ones in the Rockies near you start their climb at that altitude, like those near the mile-high city of Denver. One of our peaks, Whiteface, has a longer vertical drop than Aspen. It's also where two World Olympics were held."

"I never knew that. I guess you learn something every day."

"I always climbed alone. I could never get anyone who was in shape anyway to join me. I'm even talking about people in their twenties and thirties. One time I climbed Giant Mountain near Lake Placid. On the way up, I noted another peak on the map which I could get under my belt for the goal of becoming a Forty-sixer, those who could prove they climbed them all. It cost me time though, well past sunset on the way back."

"Not a problem with a new flashlight and fresh batteries. But because of my late start, I was moving fast and needed a break which was rarely taken. So I sat on a rock, flicked off the light and got buried in darkness of the blackest kind. Once rested, I turned on the flashlight."

"To my horror, it was dimming as I directed it at a tree. I freaked with the knowledge that suddenly my life was in real danger. I had heard a pack of coyotes ripping up some prey on Giant Mountain earlier. I also picked up the sound of something large just before I got to this resting spot. It was a startled bear ambulating down the trail. I knew this because I had come upon one in the day time climbing at Lake George. I could hear the impact of its paws on the duff."

"And you're all alone? Did you have a weapon of some kind?"

"Not even a knife on this hike because I didn't expect to climb the other mountain. I knew I had to get as much out of that light as I could by rushing down toward the trailhead but along the way it died. Angry with myself, I stubbornly pressed on trying to feel my way down the last mile of trail. Foolish might be the better description because at one point I stepped onto thin air, free-falling without a parachute to points unknown. I always wanted to sky dive but not like this."

"Hold it, are you telling me you stepped off a cliff?"

"That's exactly what I'm telling you, hundreds of feet, not quite as high as the one next to us. It's above Chapel Pond on Route 73 near St. Hubert's. Next thing I knew I hit something and lost consciousness. See that little tree that looks more like a shrub clinging to the hillside over there?" Linda followed my finger in the direction I was pointing and nodded. "That's what saved me."

"I'm not sure I'm following you. A tree broke your fall?"

"Call it another miracle, but it's true. I don't know how long I was blacked out but when I came to, I found myself on a tree jutting out from the side of that cliff and tangled in a web of scraggly branches. I had no idea who I was or what just happened. First, I checked to make sure my privates were okay."

"I already know the answer to that, but go on. This is pretty intense."

"Then I wiped the blood that was not dry from my face to see a gray panorama before me and a few homes lit up on the opposite mountainside. I realized where I was when two headlights directly below my dangling feet caught my eye. It was a car headed toward Lake Placid."

"Wow! I thought those things only happened in the movies. And you're here to tell about it."

"Oh it's a true story, I can assure you, but being the macho man I thought I was, I decided to play cliff hanger by hoisting my body up the distance I fell using tree roots for a ladder. I never would've attempted it in daylight. The height alone would have seized up my muscles. A trail rescue would've been the smart thing to wait for, but my pride derailed better judgment."

"I think my judgment is that I should take advantage of you tonight. I mean you're gonna die anyway at this rate, so why shouldn't I take advantage of that body while I still can? Let's go out in style, Lee. It's our last night together and boy what a night we could make it."

"Can we keep focused for the moment Lynn? You keep asking about my background and I'm doing the best I can to answer."

"No, I got it Lee, your background and all. But can you just show me again how you hoisted yourself up that ledge? When you raised your arms, those biceps were very convincing."

"Alright, you're not even paying attention. Is this your way of seducing me?"

She did not respond right away. Instead she simply smiled, kicked off her heels and raised one of her silky stocking legs between mine underneath our table. Reflexively I clasped it with my knees and realized just then that this might be something totally out of my intellectual control.

"Alright counselor, here we are on our own romantic cliff, and you gotta be all serious again. Trust me, you ain't falling off this one. I'll make sure of it. Plus, there's an amber moon rising."

"Didn't you see the sign at the entrance Lynn? Sex is prohibited under the tables here."

"Good one Lee. Okay, back to your story. I got a question. Did you get any more visions of your future girls on that ledge?"

"No, they were no longer unborn. They were already on the earth, but I did think of them. It sure gave me the motivation you're asking about, some bigger purpose for my existence. There had to be some reason why my life was spared so unexpectedly."

"Or maybe you were put on that mountain to figure that out, to be tested for the challenges that were coming your way. I mean, that flashlight and batteries were brand new. Go figure."

"Yeah, I guess. I'm really glad I told you this story after all, to get your take on it if nothing else. Very insightful."

"So your girls are more important than your career, that's obvious. I don't want to revisit a sore subject, but you gotta support them somehow. You gonna keep trying for your license back?"

"I never actually lost it. My license was suspended. It's been over seven years now while they find all kinds of trivia to oppose reinstatement to my civil rights practice. Trust me when I say my case broke all the records for censorship and insanity."

"What do you mean? Tell me."

"The best way I can distill all the complexities is by calling it a miscarriage of justice fueled by double standards. For example, when I learned that my secretary was setting me up for ethics violations, inside crimes influenced by my adversaries, I defended myself as a crime victim."

"Well that only makes sense."

"But they didn't see it that way. The Third Department licensing court fell back on my supervisory responsibilities. However that was before they were forced to terminate their own chief counsel and deputy lawyers in 2013 when falsified time sheets were discovered."

"You mean the lawyers for that unethical ethics committee as you called it?"

"That's right, only four weeks after my six-month license suspension. So if you follow the same standards about a duty to supervise staff, that entire bench should have been suspended for six months with years of reinstatement applications to improve their managerial skills. I mean what did they expect of me, to stand next to my secretary all day and make sure she didn't tamper with mail or phone calls? And their subordinates were the standard-bearers of lawyer ethics!"

"The same ones who are supposed to prevent over-billing practices of their colleagues, right?"

"Exactly, the foxes watching the chicken coop. I used that argument at an ethics hearing in June, 2015. It infuriated the presiding judge because I had asked that it be opened to the public and videotaped by Dr. Joseph Sorge, founder of Divorce Corp, a nationwide reform group."

"Really? I heard about that group."

"But this hearing was extraordinary, and these are secret tribunals. I was sure this one was set up to finish me off with a disbarment. Seven years of suspension, five overtime, and another seven years of disbarment. That's fourteen years minimum before I could practice law again without any crime or malpractice in thirty years of professional activity. Yeah, they were very spiteful."

"What about all your clients?"

"Most were referred out, many found substitutes, and the junior lawyer in my office took on the smaller stuff before they took him out too. Some still call me for help, and the rest could find no trustworthy options. These retaliators were brazen with no one to hold them accountable."

"Their hearing had all the drama of a public lynching," I continued. "Members of the lawyer committee had assembled in the rows behind me in court, and because it was opened to the public, the balcony was packed with young professionals. I think they were all interns or law school students anxious to see how a lawyer gets disbarred."

"You must have been out of your skin!"

"I can't even describe what I was feeling. Anyway, the justices were announced, everyone in the courtroom rose, were seated, you know, all the usual decorum and perfunctory exchanges. Then the arguments got started. It climaxed while I was detailing my status as a crime victim being treated as a criminal by the committee behind me, and I turned to point at them."

"You got to be kidding me. What did they do?"

"They did nothing, maybe turned shades of red, but not as red as the presiding judge after he cut me off with a question I'm sure he regrets to this day. That Committee was appointed by this very court as were the ethics lawyers who carried out their witch hunt, so he tried to justify their treatment of me by asking if I recognized my ethical duty to supervise my law office staff."

"I can't believe it. So they're all in bed together, just like they say online. If they work for the judges, where's the impartial decision maker?"

"The very question I posed which has never been answered to this day. I took that question all the way to the Supreme Court. They never even accepted it for review. Anyway, I'm a trial lawyer and couldn't help myself. I got my winning argument handed to me on a silver platter by the presiding judge himself on this elite panel. He had no idea what was coming his way."

"What happened, what happened?" Linda repeated impatiently.

"Well I hesitated, thought about my answer and then unleashed despite the repercussions. With all due respect, I opened, and repeated for emphasis, I absolutely agreed with the presiding judge because my ethical duty to supervise my law office staff was the same as his ethical duty to supervise the ethics lawyers they terminated for falsifying their time sheets."

"You could've heard a pin drop after that Lynn. I think there was a collective gasp from the hoard of understudies in the balcony. The best part of it is that Joe got it all on videotape. The arguments were anti-climactic after that. We all went home uncertain of an outcome."

"Then a week later I got it in the mail. The court retroactively dismissed the ethics petition with a result referred to my confidential file. I was not disbarred and remained a member of the bar paying dues and still not allowed to practice, a sort of purgatory for conscientious lawyers."

"I could not even imagine something like that," Linda interjected. "John Grisham would have a field day with it. And then there's your custody and support debacle still being dragged out."

"Yup, sometimes twice a month for over ten years as the witches on the Committee monitored the family court process for anything they could exploit. When the fix is in, it's in, nothing you can do about it. They're evil because they can be."

"I still can't figure out how you didn't go bonkers?"

"They simply assumed I did, anything to discredit my public

message. Genetics and upbringing might be the explanation. Physical fitness, good sleep and eating habits helped. Making the best of it with laughter, good friends and a healthy dose of Budweiser did too. I told you how my dad survived in a Nazi camp by drinking urine off the floor. If it wasn't for his short stature, I probably wouldn't be here today. So if he could survive that, I can survive this… I think."

"That's just amazing. I read all about the horrible war, but this was real for you. He must have had a few stories to tell."

"Yeah he did. I still remember them vividly at our kitchen table late at night. He tells one about a group of his fellow prisoners escaping a Nazi work camp. They eventually made their way into France where an elderly farm couple hid them in a barn. When the American army was spotted during the liberation campaign, my dad was returned to fight for the allies."

"So he was fighting since the beginning. Why didn't he just go the other way, settle in Paris?"

"He was fighting for his native country, Poland. Some of the best fighter pilots in the Royal Air Force were Polish. They escaped from the first blitzkrieg. This is where the earliest dogfights gave them needed skills. Most of the planes in Poland were destroyed on the ground like those at Pearl Harbor. The Japanese had a similar surprise tactic. But the success numbers in the air were quite good for the Polish pilots in 1939. They don't tell you that in western history classes."

"What did you mean by short stature, how did that help your dad survive?"

"Fate I'm sure, with the same sort of creativity I used to keep the dogs at bay here even if they are wearing robes or carrying briefcases. At first, he had been without food or water for days locked in a barn. Then one day a guard patrol opened the doors to get volunteers for road repair. My dad was short, so he dropped to the floor and was able to crawl to the front and got picked."

"You'd think the bigger guys would win the battle for that opening Lee. But maybe their bigger bodies were too weak."

"Maybe, but if he didn't have that burst of energy, like I did with that anchor, I wouldn't be here either, driving you crazy and fighting judicial persecution. The rest never made it out alive."

"You don't drive me crazy, Lee, even if you are crazy. I would've loved to meet your dad."

"Thanks, he was admired by friends, family and union members at the Special Metals steel mill. What a retirement party they had for him. But when he first came here, I think the naturalization instructors forgot to tell him about our Eighth Amendment. Okay, it applies to government and not parents, but he sure was an expert in cruel and unusual punishment. I guess that was his way of preparing me for the bizarre punishment the judges inflicted on me later on in life."

"What did he do, Lee? I feel so bad for you now."

"Let's just say I ran away from home at age six or seven. They even had an APB out for me. My mom was panic-stricken. I never thought about how it would freak her out, but I walked many miles to the zoo at the highest point of our city. They actually had a ski slope there. Something about animals and summits made me feel safe I guess. It's kinda like what I'm doing here."

"Please don't tell me you think of me as some kind of primate on this cliff?"

"Yes I do, it's why we get along so well." I answered her with a smile, but it earned me a kick under the table. "Okay, at least when you're seducing me in your animalistic way. But seriously, even animals abide by the laws of nature. In our world today, everything is getting upended at a record pace, beyond what we can humanly endure. Medicated people are everywhere."

"You got that right. On a related note, in our many talks, you put a lot of blame on judges…"

"Yeah, because we trust them more than anyone else to dispense justice."

"I know that, but what about lawyers, did you have any interesting clashes with them?"

"Too many to recite but remember, judges are lawyers on the bench. Many abused their clients as I have proven. You really think judges care about a complaint against their colleagues? So who ya gonna call, lawyer-busters? Anyway, one lawyer comes to mind if you want to hear it."

"Like I said, we've got all evening. I can stay at this romantic place talking all night."

"We've been doing that a lot lately and I can't say the managers appreciate it."

"So I'll leave the tip this time, one they will definitely appreciate. Go on."

"I was representing a woman alleging sexual harassment against her employer. It was one of the first such cases in our region which was filed in federal court but not in front of Gary Sharpe. We were litigating in the early 1990s when Justice Clarence Thomas was being scrutinized by Congress during his Supreme Court nomination process. At that time, victims had no jury right and our case was dismissed by Judge David Hurd after a trial by court." [47]

"I promptly appealed to the federal appeals court in Manhattan. By unanimous decision, it reversed Judge Hurd on grounds that he had ignored some of the most disgusting advances alleged against the

[47] Currie v Kowalewski, 810 F. Supp. 31 (NDNY 1993)

177

employer which my client, a woman supervisor, had presented at our trial."

"Be specific, what kind of advances?" Linda interrupted.

"That's not important for my story. You can read the opinion. Anyway, on remand, Judge Hurd did not conduct a new trial. Instead, he issued a replacement decision on the same trial record, this time in favor of my client. It was a highly unusual move, but the lack of a jury allowed it since the decisionmaker was the same. She was awarded money damages and attorney fees." [48]

"That must've gotten a lot of publicity at the time," Linda surmised.

"Unsolicited publicity. Front page headlines described it as a judge who reversed his own sexual harassment decision, and the employer was needlessly humiliated in three public decisions. [49] I blamed it on a greedy, arrogant lawyer who handled his defense when this could have been settled at a fraction of the harm to both sides."

"About a year or so later," I continued, "the same employer was mentioned in my office by a client during an unrelated consultation. He happened to be a friend of this employer. I sent him back with the message that his lawyer was the real cause for his combined injuries."

"In a remarkable turn of events, I was then retained by the loser to bring a malpractice action against his former lawyer. That lawyer became represented by another lawyer in that action, and we proceeded to take pretrial testimony in my law office, known as a deposition in civil cases."

"But isn't that some kind of conflict of interest?"

"Good question, Lynn, I can see you're paying attention. No, any conflict was diluted by an original client with a long concluded case who

---

[48] Currie v Kowalewski, 842 F. Supp. 57 (NDNY 1994)

[49] Noelle Crombie, *Judge Reverses Own Sexual Harassment Decision*, Observer Dispatch, February 1, 1994

was a victim of the same lawyer. My own testimony was superfluous, and she certainly had no objection. Even the defending lawyer's attorney took no action. Besides, who else could have effectively disclosed the negligence? This was long before the targeting began. But again, we digress from your original question."

"During my interrogation of this lawyer with his former client opposite him at my conference table, response testimony would be preceded with an incendiary prefix to the effect that if I knew civil rights law, I would know this, that and the other thing about his litigation strategies."

"I did what I could to ignore his offensiveness. But every man has limits. His insults continued, so finally I intercepted one of them with the logical backslap that had he known civil rights law, he would not be sitting across from his former client in a malpractice suit."

"That was it. The lawyer's elitism got the best of him. He rose from his chair with angry words to the effect that he had had enough of me. He then proceeded around the conference table to assault me. I could not believe my fortunes at that moment. I always did want to knock out an obnoxious lawyer, how about you? Well, here was that opportunity on a silver platter."

"Most remarkable, it was all legal, a right to defend myself in my own law office with a court stenographer present. I played football in the day, stayed in shape at the gym and fought real fights in my youth among the gangs of a rough neighborhood. Instincts never die."

"I reacted by throwing Attorney Obnoxious into a book stack and lunging for him even after he hit the floor. But he slipped out from under me, ran down the hallway, and out the door with me in pursuit. You might think my receptionist would be in shock, but she later admitted how often she looked forward to another day at the office, better than the movies she had to pay for."

"I could still hear the lawyer's lawyer shouting after me that I needed to think hard about the consequences of my pursuit. Knowing that the law of self-defense disappears when the danger does, I wisely halted at the top of the stairwell. My assailant was long gone. I then returned to the conference room and we settled the case right away without further proceedings. Even his own lawyer disclosed how he despised his client all along. Now how's that for a litigation strategy?"

Not conventional, that's for sure. You know, just when I thought I heard it all from you, another wild story shows up. This lawyer sounds like he was addicted to law, not very well rounded."

"A lawyer without history or literature is a mechanic, a mere working mason; if he possesses some knowledge of these, he may venture to call himself an architect. It's my friend's quote."

I paused, peered over the cobblestone wall to note the waves crashing on rocks far below, and then something in the heavens caught my eye. "Wow, look at that moon. Do you see what I see?"

Linda joined my gaze into the night sky. "Not really, it's bright white and nearly above us now."

"But see that dark wall of clouds working its way toward it."

"Yeah, it looks like an invasion of some kind. That moon sure won't last long."

"You know most people aren't aware that our moon is actually leaving us. Each year it gets farther away. Astronomers say that humanity will not survive when it gets far enough to disrupt that gravitational balance it creates with mother earth. It's like our laws of nature and parent-child relationships. We need our children as much as they need us."

"Oh my, you are so surreal. That's earth's child up there, off to see the universe. I think I'll keep that perspective. But I see the clouds differently. They're the court predators you keep talking about. Once your girls learn the truth, those clouds will clear, and you'll see them again."

"And I think I'll keep that perspective," I responded appreciatively. "Thanks Lynn."

We watched intently as the billowing clouds made their way between mother earth and her moon. The activity around us had diminished, leaving us privately fantasizing about our own purpose for existence. Those threatening formations kept invading the sky until a full moon became half, then a quarter. Finally, it was gone.

I was gone by week's end. Linda drove me to Charles de Gaulle Airport where my fugitive life began and then I was off into the wide blue yonder. I'm not sure what we had accomplished, but I did know this, it was our moment in time, a reckoning of sorts, one that would radiate to eternity or extinguish like a candlelight into cosmic dust. Either way, that moment was ours.

I never saw Linda after that. My efforts to contact her got nothing in return. As I look back though, I wondered if her true reason for saving me was to save herself, to secure a soulmate at her side when life ended, as it will for the rest of us. I guess I'll never know. But I did get a letter after I touched down at JFK. The envelope showed that it originated in Hong Kong and read:

Lee,

I wish I could be with you right now, talking into the night at Santorini, debating our issues on the Riviera or even running for cover in Paris, but I know that will never be. Don't ever change, and live every day like it's your last. That's what I learned from our romantic adventure. It's one I will cherish forever. Thanks for caring, protecting and inspiring me. And being honest. I'll always love you.

Lynn

CHAPTER 12

NO PLACE LIKE HOME

There's no place like home. Much as that phrase has been used up in countless settings, it certainly applied to me when I returned from Paris. Although my whistleblower odyssey had taken me to fascinating places, I was always happy to relax in the only one that truly mattered.

Unfortunately, due to the uncertain fate of my home, I had made no major improvements. It was the first sanctuary for my daughters, but they hadn't been here in years, which also made any relaxation bittersweet. This home was now much more than human shelter, it had taken on a life of its own, a redefinition of purpose to advance a cause for liberty. It became a sufficient garrison against a decade long blitzkrieg, and it kept my fledgling daughter relationships alive.

Of all the property and liberties seized from me, this one alone survived the onslaught in a most inexplicable way. For starters, in 2012, the ex filed a show cause petition predicated on that 2010 support order. It sought to enforce a sale provision based on eighteen months of delinquencies. At our first appearance, I offered to defeat that petition in two minutes. Intrigued by my novel proposition, the presiding judge who signed the show cause component allowed it.

The exchange was brief but quite intense because the newly assigned judge had already opened with dire warnings and a presumptuous view of my substantial arrears. My cavalier challenge was therefore a risky test of his stern demeanor. I simply relied on the express terms of that 2010 order signed by this judge's supreme court predecessor. It incorporated all prior arrears into a revised payment plan with assets apart from the home necessarily excluded from enforcement.

When the state tax department seized both of my automobiles contrary to that order, the sale proceeds were applied to my support obligations. I therefore argued that this violation operated as a prepayment beyond the monthly amounts then due. My two minutes had not yet expired, but after some head scratching, this judge could not counter my logic without risking complicity. The petition was dismissed with my ex again made liable for a hefty attorney fee. She stormed out and shifted strategy by filing in a more sympathetic family court, also known as forum shopping.

In the same year, a bank commenced a foreclosure action on the same home. Such an action was typically indefensible, and I had already made plans for relocation. But only weeks before a pretrial hearing for early eviction, I uncovered a fatal defect in the mound of documents served on me. Events followed that cannot be detailed here due to a confidentiality clause. Suffice it to say, public records will show an order ending the action in 2018 with my continued ownership.

The fate of that home was further tested by a property tax foreclosure together with my fugitive status on multiple occasions which would have prevented any defenses on my part. Moreover, whenever that home was threatened, a patriotic party would boldly step up to aid my cause. I found allies where they were least expected, some from within my adversaries' strongholds. The home elicited this sort of miraculous intervention where no other asset did. And it included a successful resistance to natural forces of which I could not possibly have played a role.

For example, on one occasion, I had decided to return one day early from a road trip. As I progressed up my long driveway, I was alerted to a growing burn odor reeking from that home. I quickly traced it to a motion detector that was too hot to touch. An overloaded circuit had failed to trigger a breaker and a fire was still threatening inside the walls. I deactivated the detector but waited tenuously. The entire structure should have gone up in flames given its remote location.

On another occasion, it was pure fate that I checked early on the clothes in my dryer. A defect in that appliance led to a small fire progressing up my cellar wall. If it were not for the early check and the cement of that wall, this fire would have gotten out of control had I come down any later. The firehouse was too distant to salvage much at all. There were also hornets' nests in the attic and outer walls with tree collapses that managed to dodge this home during freak storms.

As I toured the premises upon my return from Paris, I once again took note of the memorabilia on my entertainment center which still commemorate the birthday parties, school activities, campaign parades and exciting excursions that captured my daughters' childhoods. The playground is now saturated with vegetation, the toy room frozen exactly in the condition it was left, and the trampoline now serves as shelter for a family of deer nestled beneath it. I still shovel the snow piles off in case my girls return someday for a trip down memory lane.

Even if they don't, there are boxed-up toddler clothing, infant paraphernalia, diverse artistry and barbie dolls that continue to occupy my attic ever ready to strike up fond events. Occasionally during a clean-up routine, I ponder the notion of discarding them altogether.

Maybe a final good-bye at a garage sale. But I pull back every time I see Kristen or Cassandra in their midst.

The visions are surreal. I see each one reaching for her first animated buddy in the super saucer. A nursery play station next to it is not more than four feet high, and I can hear my eldest boasting her first daring feat of climbing to its roof top. It was a climb eclipsed many times over during our last summer together when I took them up in a parasail high above Lake George. Their surprise adventure, forever captured on video, is more than a thousand words can convey here.

These things that mean nothing to others meant everything to me in my *daddy's little girls museum*. I can still hear their laughter, the crying when someone got hurt, the girlish giggling, arguing and happy faces, indeed all the things that made our relationships so special in the day. Now I do not even know what kind of vehicle they're driving, who their first boyfriends might be, what college they will be attending, or anything meaningful about them for that matter.

To think that the government I so trusted could kill all this without cause of any kind. It still infuriates me after all that time away on the lam. A slew of sadistic lawyers in robes would not be here to share in all the devastation. But they were aberrant strangers, the fact that the mother of these same little girls could commit such a heinous murder of parent-child relationships was beyond any moral comprehension.

How could this mother sleep soundly after knowing the truth of it all? How could she simply carry on as if nothing had happened? How could she continue to deny her role in all this? How could she incessantly brainwash her daughters against their own dad, how could she place money above the interests of that only dad, and how could she actively recruit father substitutes while making the real dad pay for the kidnapping? Pure evil, it was the blatant work of Satan himself.

The tactics employed to systematically terminate parent-child relationships under the prevailing custody framework are virtually infinite. As summarized in Chapter Two, anything can be used to influence a referral for forensic evaluations. Forensic simply means evidence in the way of opinions that are admitted in court to assist in custody decisions, and there are growing types of evaluations that can be exploited to turn a few months into years of costly litigation.

In my case, the parent adversary was following the custody playbook and tactics recommended by her several lawyers over the years. Evaluations were a big one because once placed on the defensive through the most incredulous or unsubstantiated allegations, a victim could be forever hounded to a point where he or she is simply forced to walk away prior to any timely set trial. Effectively this forecloses due process since the standard of review for a forensic referral is merely sound discretion. A parent could be involuntarily ousted from court on cost alone.

To be sure, at a 2019 reform conference in Washington D.C., I cited a series of forensic referrals that cost one parent $50,000, following with the assumption that such figures were on the high side. Afterward, another victim from the audience approached me privately to assert that my figure was not high at all given the quarter million he spent for the same process. We're talking about every day working class. Victims are reluctant to go public with these abuses due to a harmful stigma, and that induces judges to expand the lucrative process with impunity. [50]

To illustrate this aspect of a growing epidemic, on one occasion I was returning from a weekend with my girls at an indoor water park. As a weekend warrior, a noncustodial parent has to maximize enjoyment to offset the alienation process, and my daughters loved these excursions because we lived in snow country. The ex was busy with her anal routine

---

[50] New York has now brought pets into play. No lawyer fee impact was assessed during legislative deliberations, Whittaker, *Bill requires court to mull pets' interests in custody cases*, Jamestown Post Journal, June 8, 2021.

of texting me whenever I was running late. It did not matter that her girls had enjoyed such a wonderful time with their dad. To the contrary, this custodial parent was likely incensed by it.

It got so anal that I texted back that I was in Rio to make up for all my deprived parenting time, my way of saying enough is enough. It was pathetically obvious that this was a facetious text as it was sent from her driveway, and she could verify the girls' exiting my vehicle from her picture window. Nevertheless, to my utter shock, I was hauled into family court days later to defend against a show cause order limiting my geographic activity to two local counties.

Incredibly, a hearing was actually held on the Rio caper in May, 2011 with my children's assigned lawyer questioning, quite astoundingly, whether I was truly in Rio while dropping off his "clients." I refused to answer on "stupidity" grounds despite the judge's directive to respond. My refusal was then used against me with our first forensic evaluations ordered of mom and dad. Supervision was later imposed. More on that under the subject "forensic funny farm."

Other playbook antics included the scheduling of discretionary activities on weekends. The rationale used here was that these were extensions of school-related events that truncated my parenting time. Sometimes my entire period would be preempted by events in other states where I was remanded to observer status. Ever the schemer, this abuser would then convey privately, and contrary to court order, that I was not interested in the girls or their activities. A secret bond was established which lasted to the time when all contact had ended. Even a senile judge could discern the alienation agenda, but each one I petitioned would find a way of excusing it.

I was a fairly resilient and creative victim, so I offset these tactics as best I could. For example, my girls loved playgrounds, so to save on travel time, I had an elaborate one built in my yard. When I was denied two years of 'trick or treat' routines, I took the event to my home on a non-Halloween day where I posted friends in costumes at 'scary stations' around the grounds. I invited my girls' classmates and friends to join with their parents. We concluded with treats and a cake after a magic show by Leon Etienne who would later achieve notoriety in Las Vegas.

At the end of each weekend, I would make it a practice to quiz the girls on their favorite experiences. I also replayed them on video camera. They included educational ones to such places as Saratoga Historic Battlefield. These offsets were designed to solidify sound memories. But even those memories were erased over time. It was all a part of Satan's Docket as I called it, and my case may stand on record as the first to request an exorcism of the custodial parent. This was intended to emphasize the absurdity of a highly abused forensic evaluation process.

Conventional thinking would place the cause for all this under the heading of severe parental alienation syndrome. But that was a psychological model made popular by Dr. Richard Gardner during the 1980s. Nearly four decades later, it had yet to achieve validity by his profession or a place in the DSM-5 manual. That may be explained, at least in part, by citing the right church but the wrong pew, because this was not a psychological disorder but a human rights violation. Parental alienation was a symptom, not the underlying cause as I had been urging.

There are so many more questions that remain unanswered. But it's not like the alienator here had anything real to cite as justification. There was no child protection report, no incident to support such depravity, and all her offense petitions had been thrown out. Prison felons were being treated better. So after fifteen years of anal jousting, what was it all about? I was near millionaire status when she started this in 2006. My girls today would have wanted for nothing.

Deep down, if she had a conscience, Kelly Hawse-Koziol would finally admit that she had lied her way to that almighty custody award, one that I never even cared to vie for. I only wanted to spend more time with my girls. Like so many fires she ignited, she still did not know how to put this one out. And no matter how she tries to bury it today, it is a forest fire that will haunt her to her dying days. Such is the sad ending of so many who trusted this custody regime.

It is a regime that can turn a parent into a brutal killer overnight. Recent examples include a mother who was convicted of murdering her two-year old daughter rather than comply with a custody change order that was not timely enforced. She was also convicted of attacking police with two knives when they arrived. [51] Another featured an NYPD officer charged with murdering his autistic eight-year old son in January, 2020 by leaving him overnight in a freezing garage. [52] In 2019, a mother purchased a gun overnight and killed her estranged husband and two children. [53] According to an investigative report, 725 such deaths were suppressed by a state agency. [54]

Court induced carnage can occur directly by use of a weapon, but it can also occur indirectly through a recklessly created environment that causes a death much like a drunk driver, concealed hole in the ground, or a cancer causing ingredient in a product. The indirect means was the one used against me, and judicial arrogance fueled it. As stated, the reckless and even malicious persecution of me consisted of a combination of abuses over many years.

---

[51] *'You Are In A Special Category Of Evil': Mamaroneck Mom Who Killed 2-Year-Old Daughter Sentenced to 25 Years To Life*, newyork.cbslocal.com, October 31, 2019

[52] Mongelli & Musumeci, *Michael Valva, NYPD cop charged in son's murder, tears up in court as 911 call played*, New York Post, May 11, 2021

[53] *Mother Charged with murders of husband, 2 children in Tacony*, ABC 7 (Philadelphia), October 18, 2019

[54] Chris Bragg, State agency suppressed 725 child death reports over decade, Times Union, October 13, 2020

Five years after my return from Paris, I was rushed to an emergency room at Albany Medical Center for a life-threatening condition. During my stay, and despite the custodial parent's full knowledge, this mother actually filed for yet another support warrant. My girls never even called to see how I was doing. Now how evil can it get after all the sacrifices I had made for them?

The best that I could learn from some of the medical experts is that my years of persecution provided a good explanation for my condition. Severe stress and anxiety over an extended period can wreak havoc on a person's health and longevity. I was told that my condition might never have been discovered through regular doctor visits, providing a serious cautionary note for those who believe they are impervious to family court abuses.

During a two year period leading up to my hospitalization I had been subjected to a "shoot-on-sight" support warrant and later, a beating by state police at a sobriety checkpoint after they learned of my identity. That incident also landed me in the emergency room while elevating many times the stress I was subjected to pending a resolution during a pandemic that was delaying speedy outcomes. It is now the subject of a civil rights claim.

This checkpoint calls to mind a prophetic statement I made in a June 12, 2015 report to then U.S. Attorney General Loretta Lynch. Prior to her elevation to that post by President Barack Obama, she was one of those who testified along with me at the Moreland Commission on Public Corruption. It focused on the true cause for the police murder of Walter Scott in South Carolina on April 4, 2015. He was the black father shot dead five times in the back by a white cop while fleeing unarmed from a child support warrant at a traffic stop.

This report included a presentation I made to national media and Congressman James Clyburn at Scott's funeral. I outlined how the killing was fueled by Title IV-D incentive funding. I was promised a meeting at the Capitol, but it never materialized despite follow-ups. Very telling, the child support aspect of this tragedy was so protected that the incident is rarely emphasized in publications. When it is, the focus is typically on that hung jury during the state criminal prosecution of the traffic cop, not a child support bureaucracy that was now killing for money.

I also emphasized in my 2015 report how I was being targeted and could end up like Walter Scott. Even I doubted my own predictions until 2018 when that dangerous suspect bulletin was added to a support warrant and leaked unlawfully to the media. Two years after that, the sobriety checkpoint might have turned fatal if I fled the scene on a conditional license violation based on support arrears. I was interrogated instead on suspicion of a DUI conditional license violation.

The state police who pounded me to the pavement at that scene were visibly offended by my discovered background as a civil rights attorney only two months following the George Floyd murder. During an extended detainment they were likely reminded of that earlier secret bulletin. On July 31, 2020, they piled on top of me with a combined weight exceeding 500 pounds. Breathing constraints prompted me to compare my treatment to George Floyd.

That plea from the bottom of the pile produced resounding laughter. No mention of it is made in later incident summaries filed by those officers. Only one month earlier, in response to the Floyd protests, New York Governor Andrew Cuomo signed into law a mandate for all state police to wear body cameras. No such devices, not even every-day smart phone recording, were present at this prearranged scene. There were also no media reports, news releases or public access to the site despite my transport to the emergency room and internal affairs visit at the hospital.

Meanwhile all neighboring and overlapping police agencies had been using body cams. One of them recorded an extended beating of an arrestee in Utica, New York only weeks after my incident in the same city. That cop was immediately suspended and the relevant recording featured on the city's website. The Walter Scott murder was already being covered up with false reports in 2015 until days later when a concealed by-stander released a phone video of the event.

At least one device could have been used at this highly regulated checkpoint involving countless motorists. If the disregard of laws by New York's elite police agency can be blamed on funding, why should the citizen follow laws prohibiting burglary when funding is unavailable to buy groceries? With all this, and more at stake, one would expect an aggressive prosecution. Instead, all charges were dismissed or never pursued to conviction. This was likely prompted by a breath test that was too low for legal admission into evidence. So they buried the whole incident. [55]

How it all got to this alarming point is now the rest of this story. Hindsight, Linda may have been right after all. If I had stayed on the run, my ongoing demise could have been reversed. Like Edward Snowden, I could have started a new life. With all the global terrorism, no one would have put up any roadblocks for child support. But for the sake of the general public, and parents in particular, the roadblocks I did endure remain a critical learning curve for any reform effort.

In the blockbuster film, *The Patriot*, Captain Benjamin Martin,

---

[55] This may also be explained by "systemic racism" later exposed in a timely story by the Associated Press. It gave examples of discriminatory treatment at traffic stops, a sarcastic, racist poster in a superior's office, and a 28 year veteran who is now pursuing a civil rights action for multiple uses of racial slurs by his supervisor. This elite agency's racist history adds to this author's mistreatment as a civil rights attorney and concealment from public knowledge, see (AP) Mustian and Fassett, *Still on the Farm*, (Utica) Observer Dispatch, June 8, 2021.

played by actor Mel Gibson, warns the South Carolina Assembly that "An elected legislature can trample a man's rights as easily as a King can." That foreboding has real world application in the ordeal I sustained after challenging the oppressive laws put into place by Congress and our state legislators regarding custody and child support. Spineless politicians kissing up to special interests have imposed a series of burdens trampling a parent's liberty rights without concern for their combined impact.

Such burdens were thrust upon me to a level which made it impossible to maintain any kind of employment or child relationship. At the same time, the jurists who benefitted from incentive grants were crafting evidentiary substitutes to fictionalize an economic condition that still required me to pay support obligations at inflated law practice levels. Reality was disregarded so that the state could record maximum support collections. This agenda is applied without concern for child access, leading to resistance, carnage and little or no achievement of stated objectives.

To advance funding goals, state legislatures have enacted laws that require courts to name a "custodial parent" as a condition for a valid divorce or support agreement. Typically, an opt-out clause allows parents to by-pass the mandatory support formula, but to do so requires them to engage in a comparative analysis which often dilutes the reality of this option.

There is also collaborative law, but such processes are similarly diluted by additional attorneys who cannot be used later if agreement fails. More lawyers are added to a two-tiered process to support the adage that any community which cannot support one lawyer can always support two.

Here is a partial listing of fictions, in addition to those provided earlier, that were orchestrated over the years to maximize funding at the expense of judicial impartiality and due process:

1) Service of a support violation petition can be achieved by simple mailing. These petitions typically contain boldface, capital letter warnings of arrest and incarceration. If this type of service is challenged on due process grounds, it can incur the cost of personal service unlike criminal counterparts which these proceedings resemble.

2) Expedited case management rules can provide a mere thirty days for defense preparation between a first appearance and trial. All too often, a jail term for contempt of a support order is the standard outcome conditioned on a purge or payment amount. Satisfaction is routinely coerced from relatives, employers or friends.

3) The case for a violation and jail term is easily made by a single non-party witness, typically a social services employee offering a delinquent support summary into the record. Intent is presumed from its mere production without any other proof.

4) The burden of proof is wrongfully shifted to the defending party to prove innocence. The standard for conviction is the lowest of all forms of litigation despite the stigma and incarceration which are at stake. There is no jury or indigent right to counsel.

5) Support judges have invented an evidentiary substitute known as imputed income which assures the highest support obligation possible, often well beyond the realistic income capacities of the targeted debtor. Defending parties are treated at higher levels of income based on past employment reports even when wrongfully terminated.

6) Support obligations continue to accrue at regular intervals during incarceration for violations or any other reason. They also accrue when a father is later found not to be a biological parent and despite frauds used to deny him child access. They

also accrue until a petition for recourse is actually filed despite its futility in a biased process.

7) The state has expanded its tyrannical power beyond the original objective of recouping welfare costs for abandoned mothers on public assistance. It now acts as representative for self-sufficient support seekers to create a serious imbalance in the scales of justice. Attorney fees and other costs are made a part of the final judgment.

In my case, all but the actual incarceration was used against me. But the many processes employed were also fraught with serious error, gender prejudice and whistleblower retaliation. At what point, then, is a victim pushed to such an extreme that our Constitution confers upon him a legal right to fight back or take the so-called law into his own hands?

You be the jury.

CHAPTER 13

SHOW TRIALS IN THE GOLDMINE

Without repeating the persecution detailed in earlier chapters, the judges who dominated my family proceedings over the years could be satirically described as the Sadistic Seven. Supreme Court Justice Abe Fortas once compared these tribunals to kangaroo courts (Chapter One). But the better depiction in my ordeal was a series of show trials. This species of proceedings is often traced to Soviet purges and the People's Court of Nazi Germany. Basic due process is replaced by insults, threats and state propaganda spewed from petty tyrants on the bench.

Politician James "Bond" Tormey is the administrative judge who made all the judge assignments including the Sadistic Seven. Remember he's the guy sued by his chief family court clerk due to unlawful treatment for her refusal to conduct "political espionage" beyond her job description. She recovered $600,000 after retaliatory assignments to the same far-away places as my cases were sent. I was denied such recourse because judges are still immune from litigant lawsuits.

One of my support cases was assigned to state supreme court judge, Michael Daley, as an "Acting Family Court Judge" and my custody case was assigned to a family court judge, Martha Walsh-Hood, as an "Acting Supreme Court Judge." This really did happen. To this day,

I still cannot figure out how it came about especially after Tormey removed Daley previously from my custody case and returned it to the original divorce judge, John Grow. I was blamed as a result.

Judge Daley was set to confirm a willful support violation on May 26, 2009. It was found against me by a non-elected hearing magistrate, George Getman, a/k/a, G. Stephen Getman, who had been suspended as an attorney for a mere six months after admitting to misappropriation of more than $7,000 in client money. [56] He denied my pre-decision motion for his removal from my case.

I was not physically present at the Daley confirmation hearing due to the set-up I was logically perceiving, a jail term ambush. Instead, I called in by phone from a location near Canada. On the hearing transcript that day, prior to my call, Judge Daley opened with a bombastic pitch that he was somehow assigned to this support case and he "did not know how it got here."

This may have been nothing more than a deflection to feign an impartial tribunal. Moments later, I called in and immediately challenged Judge Daley's authority while reminding him of a motion which had been filed for his disqualification. That motion was based on his earlier removal from a highly politicized client case which made Daley look bad. I also raised his presence as a violation of subject matter jurisdiction, supported by his own record statement that there was no order authorizing his assignment to a limited jurisdiction court. I would later argue this in federal court to strip Daley of judicial immunity, but that was never even referenced in the outcomes. [57]

Daley's prior removal in the client case resulted in dismissal of a six count indictment contrary to a guilty plea he had been instigating.

---

[56] Matter of G. Stephen Getman, 147 AD 2d 163, 542 NYS 2d 896 (4th Dept 1989)
[57] Stump v Sparkman, 435 US 349 (1978)(Judge is stripped of immunity if he acts in clear absence of jurisdiction)

Like the typical show trial, that made him judge and prosecutor (his prior position). A jury and replacement judge saved my client's career. In parting remarks on that record, Judge Daley assured that he would share my "histrionics" with a replacement judge in his county where fortunately the case was not reassigned.

So if you still don't believe that judges talk behind the scenes to target critics, here you have a public declaration showing that they do. Daley never did set up a hearing on my later recusal motion as promised on the record, but he did violate me months afterward in a decision with no mention of the foregoing. As stated earlier, it led to my first license suspension on February 5, 2010. The media learned of it before I did, and the news was front page for two successive days.

At the end of the telephonic transcript of May 26, 2009, Judge Daley concludes that he had always found me to be respectful and courteous to the court. So here we have a compliment regarding my professionalism from a hostile judge who had known me for over twenty years. With that backdrop, we turn to the custody component of my ordeal which was assigned virtually overnight to Syracuse Family Judge Martha Walsh-Hood. She was meeting me for the first time.

On July 20, 2009, the parties appeared for our first custody trial. A reading of the case record would confound any legal expert and make a truly impartial judge want to adjourn proceedings just to get a better handle on things. How we went from Supreme Court to Family Court and back to Supreme Court with a family judge presiding as the eighteenth trial jurist is perplexing enough, but familiarity with the subject matter is crucial to decisional competency on any case.

And that is what led to the unraveling of Martha's fake neutrality, her underlying bias against fathers generally and this one in particular. As this week-long custody trial progressed, it became increasingly evident that her mind had been made up. The outcome was a done deal on multiple counts no matter how much faith I supplied to our justice system, no matter how many witnesses I brought, no matter what it cost the people affected by it. By the time it was over, I would storm out of court after condemning the entire process as a giant fraud on fathers and the public.

The opening segment of trial transcript will verify the flawed structure and chaotic process which federal judge Gary Sharpe later blamed on me in a twisted 2014 decision. It can be seen how unfamiliar Martha Walsh-Hood was with the record, an arguable due process violation, yet she pressed forward anyway with excuses. Short cut explanations are found within parentheses.[58]

Walsh-Hood: *Okay, good morning. Well, I've spent some time trying to become acquainted with this rather voluminous file, and my intent in scheduling the earliest possible court date was to try and address the... some of the issues which both parties have raised in a number of different courts... Given the fact that Judge Greenwood had scheduled the matter prior to his recusal for July 20th, I readjusted my court calendar...*

(After dismissing three petitions on consent, the judge proceeded with others): With regard to the support issue, it's my understanding that (it) was originally heard, I believe, by Judge Caldwell (who never heard any issue after stepping down at the outset).

Mr. Koziol: *There were some eighteen judges on this case (2006 thru 2009)...*

Walsh-Hood: *I understand.*

Mr. Koziol: *As far as the support issues go, and the intertwined, interwoven (proceedings), having been here from the beginning, perhaps I can best speak to that history (neither the child lawyer, William Koslosky*

---

[58] Koziol v Hawse-Koziol, New York Supreme Court, Oneida County Case No. D2004-422102; Custody transcript Vol. I at pg. 2-30 (July 20, 2009)

nor mother's latest attorney, Rebecca Crance, had been present for the entire history).

Walsh-Hood: *Well, I'm not so much concerned about the history, although I did go through it. My understanding is that the support issue was in fact heard (by magistrate Getman) that there is a willful component to that hearing, that is before Judge Daley.*

Mr. Koziol: *That's correct, who was previously removed from the case, and he's back for some reason that he didn't seem to understand… I don't know how that's going to resolve itself.*

Walsh-Hood: *But from my selfish perspective… all matters relating to support are before another judge, although I do understand that under* Eschbach *and* Friederwitzer *(case precedent) in custody (decisions), support can be a factor considered… (here we see how a judge recognizes that child support comes into a custody trial through the back door even though they are supposed to be litigated separately, yet another fraud upon the public to increase funding goals). Further it's my understanding that the Judgment of Divorce (Judge Grow decision) is now on appeal as well as issues relative to, Mr. Koziol, your original request for a change of venue (change of location to a remote judicial district)… I think the venue change has actually been accomplished through a number of recusals…to be heard by the Appellate Division (already decided by it at the time). In fact there's a federal action pending for some of the same relief that's before this court…"*

Mr. Koziol: *That's right.*

Walsh-Hood: *Even given that situation… there are applications by both parties in Supreme Court and Family Court (both trial courts in New York)… both parties are seeking custody and allegations of contempt, or at least Mr. Koziol has of Mrs. Hawse-Koziol. Is that everybody's understanding?*

Mr. Koziol: *I don't know if you're characterizing it as I see it, but Ms. Hawse has been allowed to go through support court, she's gone through all that process, while my petition against her for violating parenting orders, and I want to get to this past weekend, once again I was deprived of an entire weekend with my children… For now, in terms of the narrow framework of pending petitions is concerned, it's my contempt against her that has been held in abeyance for a couple years.*

Walsh-Hood: (after denying my motions for removal of William Koslosky as Judge-Appointed Child Attorney and Walsh-Hood as presiding judge)… I don't feel there is any reason for me to step down as other judges have done. You stated yourself, very eloquently I may add, that matters have been pending in the court which have not been heard since 2007. The day has come, sir, for those matters to be litigated… if you feel uncomfortable in proceeding today, though I'm sure you are capable of doing so, then Ms. Crance (mother's lawyer) can proceed first, and that would give you a little additional time… Ms. Crance, are you willing to do that?"

Ms. Crance: Yes.

Mr. Koziol: No, Judge, I'd like to be heard.

Walsh-Hood: Sure.

Mr. Koziol: Obviously you haven't read the petition and you're making a determination before reading the content of it, which is not your fault because you were just served today.

Walsh-Hood: I was just served.

Mr. Koziol: There's a good reason for that, if you're ready.

Walsh-Hood: Go ahead.

(I explained that the past weekend was unilaterally denied for tactical reasons. I needed that time to recall events necessary for my proofs. The judge quickly interrupted to attack me only, citing improper child preparation which the ex had been doing with impunity all along with her dominant custody periods. She denied that weekend to rehabilitate bonds with the mother's parents from another state, her only witnesses. Her violation of our

custody order impaired my ability to present any kind of case. The judge replied:)

<u>Walsh-Hood</u>: *You know what I'm going to do, Mr. Koziol, before hearing your argument, I'm going to take a ten minute recess. I'm going to review your papers, and I'll allow you to be heard and then I'm going to rule on the motion.*

As expected, the motion was denied, but it can be seen how Judge Walsh-Hood was ready to start this trial without having concededly read my violation petition. Moreover, she claimed readiness to proceed without the proper first appearance or pretrial conference which sets the scope of trial ahead of time. Here in this opening interplay, Walsh-Hood is crafting her own expedited process for custody, contempt and other petitions after dismissing three on consent of the parties.

Setting aside the unprepared judge for the moment, how is a lawyer or litigant to know what proofs to present or witnesses to subpoena to a court more than fifty miles from our homes with this prejudicial change of standard procedure? She tried to justify herself by citing years of delay, but these were caused by a denied venue change and as many as eighteen prior biased judges. Rushing proceedings now proved to be a grave error because it only forced me to correct this unprepared judge as evidenced by her claim that Judge Caldwell had been substantively engaged.

This expedited trial was nothing more than a "show trial" with a predetermined outcome. It is all that was necessary to validate my challenges to a structurally flawed process under the federal child support funding statute. This judge knew exactly what I was asserting but did everything she could to protect the system. The appellate and federal judges reviewing this did the same.

Another due process anomaly is seen in the reversal of the order of presentment. As the custody petitioner, I had the benefit of starting with my case-in-chief. Instead, to make this system work, the responding party was allowed to go first. It was fatal to my case because surprise testimony such as "striking my child on one occasion," caused me to stand up and call the mother-in-law a bald-faced liar. I simply could not control my outrage over a non-existent strike of either child.

There was no such accusation ever made by anyone in the prior record, the petitions, the public or in any incident report. Even the scheming and spiteful mom, by my recollection, never made such a claim. And although the ultimate decision here did not accept that claim, it was clear that my reputation on all fronts was under attack in this one-sided hearing. Still, with each reaction, Walsh-Hood was taking copious notes on my logical emotions to support her intended outcome.

The reversal in presentment also allowed my custody adversary to derail my accurate position, unwavering for years to this point, that I wanted more time with my daughters. She lumped all of my father-daughter experiences into that standard, tactical category of avoiding child support when the litigation damage alone exceeded the total support amount due many times over. This tactic was unleashed during her opening testimony with nothing but her mouth to prove it.

The support strategy was not only a gross concoction obtained from a custody playbook, but it was countered by everything realistic, from a voluntary forty-five percent support increase offered in 2006 to a successful career in which money was never an issue, at least not until the speech retributions were inflicted. Even if we were to accept this concoction as true, why should money matter at all in a custody trial? This is where a pay-to-parent scandal comes into focus.

Anxious to feed into the stereotypes, Judge Walsh-Hood took this support avoidance concoction to an absurd level by requesting that

I stop pointing my pen in my adversary's direction when making an objection. Somehow this was intimidating to her, even though the alleged victim made no such claim. This was not only a clear showing of gender bias and the direction this case was headed, but it incited my adversary to make idiotic fear claims in later proceedings.

At the same time, the purported victim showed no fear during child exchanges or outside events, even asking me during a chance encounter at Lake George to watch our girls while she went off to get towels. Despite such testimony, none of it mattered. I struggled against a novice lawyer who repeatedly failed to lay proper foundation for her questions, i.e. dates, locations, etc. while the judge became more fixated on a writing implement than proper evidence for decision. Here is the relevant interplay which poisoned later proceedings and public safety in our courts: [59]

<u>Crance</u>: *Has Mr. Koziol relayed to you his desire to have shared or half parenting time?*

<u>Hawse-Koziol</u>: *Yes.*

Q: *Has he… what is your understanding as to why he wants shared parenting time?*

A: *So he doesn't have to pay child support.*

<u>Mr. Koziol</u>: *Have I told you that? Objection, please, can I go back? When did I say this?*

<u>Walsh-Hood</u>: *Okay, you're objecting for foundation?*

<u>Mr. Koziol</u>: *Right.*

<u>Walsh-Hood</u>: *I'm going to ask you not to point, counsel. I'm just asking you not to point.*

<u>Mr. Koziol</u>: *Your honor, I have a pen in my hand, if the record can please reflect this. I flipped the pen in her direction, I meant her, so we can*

---

[59] <u>Koziol v Hawse-Koziol</u>, New York Supreme Court, Oneida County Case No. D2004-422102; Custody transcript, Vol. II at pg. 230-233 (July 20, 2009)

find out from her. I don't understand that to be a negative or somehow an influential statement based on what we've been through.

Walsh-Hood: *Counsel, we just had testimony about a number of alleged domestic violence incidents.* [60] *You were objecting as to foundation, which is fine. You are somewhat animated at this time and you have the pen pointed. She was indicating some incidents, and I don't want her to feel intimidated. I'm not suggesting that you're trying to do that. I'm simply requesting that you not point the pen... That you were holding and taking notes, and I...*

Mr. Koziol: *In response, Judge, to make it clear so I don't get accused of that, I'm going to put my pen down, I will no longer write. That is habit.*

Walsh-Hood: *No, no I'm not suggesting that you're intentionally pointing at her, I'm asking you not point the pen, that's all, in her direction. If you want to point it in my direction, go ahead... (but not the witness)*

Mr. Koziol: *Judge, I would just like the record to reflect my understanding, I did point it in the direction of the bench and her, but I don't know how I'm animated at this point. I don't see it, but if you do, I'm going to have to leave it at that. I've been very respectful, very calm (to this witness), it's emotional... I'm non-responsive to most things here. I want that for the record because there is no video camera here.*

Walsh-Hood: *I don't believe so, though there are cameras in the hall and other places.*

---

[60] While stressing these alleged domestic incidents corroborated by no witness or independent proof, Judge Walsh-Hood was likely manufacturing her own proof here for later decision. That decision made no mention of an off-duty sheriff deputy, posted inside my home, who witnessed an assault by the mother during a child exchange. By opening the custody record to pre-divorce periods, Walsh-Hood was also able to facilitate false claims at the marital home where no witnesses were present. There was never an incident report during that remote period, and although physical abuse was never found, there was no accountability for the fabrications.

I had been litigating trials unblemished in both federal and state courts for more than twenty-three years at the time of this pen-pointing admonition. Never had I been restrained in this manner, indeed, not even in the many support, custody and violation proceedings as a pro se litigant before and after this directive. A look at the courtroom would show how the bench and witness stand were in close proximity to one another. It would therefore be nearly impossible for me to point at one and avoid the other, yet one more example of contempt by ambush.

Despite Martha's back-peddling, this was a clear anti-man edict corroborated by a court officer thereafter who advised me that Walsh-Hood had an anti-father record in Syracuse. How does one control a pen while objecting as a habit over so many years? Incidents like this were many, but exemplified here to show the uphill battle good fathers face every day in these courts and why so many of them are forced out of their children's lives. There was no finding of physical abuse in the ultimate decision, but when I stormed out at the conclusion, I will admit I was very animated.

Throughout this trial, child attorney, William Koslosky, and Walsh-Hood took issue with nearly every witness and positive aspect of my parenting time while accepting virtually everything the custodial parent offered. Even my campaign parades were attacked as an exploitation of my children who enjoyed them so much while throwing candy to others along the parade route. The shocking aspect here is that one would expect such auspicious events to be lauded in a genuine child-oriented court. Instead, in family courts, heroin addicts are being reunited with children.

One of Martha's colleagues, Family Judge Randy Caldwell (mentioned in her trial opening), paraded with his children and relatives during this same campaign year as did most candidates I knew. Indeed, I dare say, Martha herself was parading at one time alongside her dad when he campaigned for Congress. But Walsh-Hood, Judge Tormey and politically correct judges of an opposite party evidently render such "exploitation" a-okay in those identical situations.

On the last day of trial, a steady flow of provocation culminated in a seizure of my notes on the witness stand when I finally testified. Walsh-Hood had entered an order I had never experienced in any self-represented context. She wanted me to present testimony in question-answer format which I could not do under such short notice and, as stated, the lack of any pretrial conference. We compromised with a note version and exhibits necessarily taken with me to the stand.

At one point during convincing testimony, Koslosky objected on yet another anal ground of reading from my notes. That was not the case, of course, as proven by the lack of ethics charge threatened by Judge Hood on this same basis before "the Fourth Department" licensing court. Now, even the lawyers were favored as their notes were allowed. I was self-represented, but the judge began referring to me as "counsel" presumably as a predicate for such an ethics charge despite the obvious fact that I was not acting in that capacity. Obviously, I also had no client.

By the time the trial was concluding, I had no notes to convey ten years of events I could never independently recollect, my pen was now a weapon of intimidation, every anal detail about a model parent was being twisted and debated to absurdity, and my daughters had been exploited to advance a prominent career which would have benefitted them immensely. Finally, I had had enough and asked to be excused from the trial altogether. I did not come here to be abused by a gang of misfits. A judge deserves only so much respect as she reciprocates as a public servant.

After my departure from "her" court on July 24, 2009, child

attorney, William Koslosky, disclosed a domestic violence incident at his home fifty years earlier during closing statements.

What any of this had to do with my case I'll never know, but I found it buried in costly trial transcripts, a treasure trove of billable hours on behalf of grade school clients who could never hold him accountable. I also found fables, serious provocations and tales of horror.

It was abundantly clear that William Koslosky was on a mission of revenge, abusing his entrusted role and tax dollars to murder exemplary father-daughter bonds. He actually had the audacity under protection of court security to accuse me of "terrorizing" my children, an accusation which if made in my presence could have sent him out the court window. Once again, fate had spared us all a disaster due to my pre-closing departure which was then exploited. It allowed the judge to treat the mother's testimony as true even when it was pathetically otherwise.

This terrorist thing is being exploited these days by thoughtless provocateurs to advance their wallets and purses without regard for the dire consequences. Terrorists fly planes into buildings. They don't pursue proper channels for the resolution of disputes. I visited the Trade Center ruins on the day after 9-11 to volunteer what I could. Comparing me to a terrorist as Judge Gartenstein had done to Professor Pappas (Chapter 3) was an assault upon my patriotism and my fatherhood.

Apparently, William Koslosky had been using this terrorist depiction in a lot of cases because he also used it to describe his own dad. As he explained it, little Billy was "terrorized" by his police officer dad during a dinner argument a half century earlier. Somehow his dad's uniform and gun made him dangerous. His closing statement reflected a childhood contempt for that dad which he simply transferred to his latest target. You be the judge:

> *One thing that I remember is disagreement between my mom and*
> *my dad. My dad was a policeman and one day he came home and he*
> *was mad because we didn't have red-skinned potatoes and all that she*
> *could say is we have Yukon Gold, and I was terrorized. I'd never seen*
> *dad arguing like this and, my God, he's in the police uniform with a*
> *gun. What is he going to do? So I went to the store to get red-skinned*
> *potatoes and I don't like Yukon Gold.*

If there is any purpose to a judge in any proceeding, it is to control it so that sanity, justice and civility may prevail. Wide latitude is generally given to lawyers in closing statements, but in this case, it was a custody proceeding, not a high-profile murder trial. There is no way my daughters, aged five and seven at the time, would have approved of their involuntarily appointed lawyer referring to their daddy this way. It was the appointing judge's duty to prevent it. But Walsh-Hood was evidently enjoying this all with sadistic satisfaction. Another judge might have cut Billy off:

> *Mr. Koslosky, this is family court, not criminal court. What's*
> *with all the terrorism in your characterizations of an American father*
> *seeking proper relief here? There's no jury, and such colorful depictions*
> *will not influence me. I've heard and seen all the evidence as you have.*
> *There's nothing to support any of this. No child protection agency has*
> *even been contacted, let alone involved. And I could care less about*
> *your own dad and whatever went on with these potatoes. Confine*
> *yourself to the record, and let's move on, alright?*

After Walsh-Hood disqualified herself without explanation the next year, continuing proceedings were assigned to Judge Michele Pirro-Bailey. At one point, a desperate Kelly Hawse-Koziol interrupted court arguments between lawyers to announce a fear of my body language. It caused that judge to direct her to face the wall if she truly felt that way.

This is how brazen the gender card has been abused despite having all of her prior offense (fear) petitions thrown out.

This is no small matter for the general public. During the same year in the same Syracuse courthouse, I watched curiously as a security officer was escorting my adversary mother to her vehicle beyond view of the courthouse. It prompted me to investigate. While doing so, violence erupted in the hallway involving a chained inmate. Security was called in while one of them was placating a mom's custody playbook. I reported the safety issue to the court's chief officer, Judge James "Bond" Tormey. Nothing came of it other than more waste of taxpayer dollars.

Pirro-Bailey's participation in this ongoing saga defies rational explanation, and she too stepped down only months later, also without explanation. Her involvement can be summarized under the heading "forensic funny farm." She was the first to issue forensic evaluation orders of both parents. This came about once again after my premature departure from "her" court as well. I had filed an extensive cross-motion to obtain make-up time lost to a fraudulent process.

However, this judge was not about to reopen that can of worms and even admitted that she had not reviewed my papers. She went further to deny me oral argument after hearing from my opposition. For all intents, my existence was thereby erased, prompting me to exit early. Pirro-Bailey was also the judge who presided over the Rio caper. After self-disqualification, her replacement judge removed the forensic order on the same record only four months later, proving just how arbitrary and needless these orders can be, how easily they can be abused.

But like a rodent without a remedy, that decision was reversed again, this time in favor of the mother. In 2013, Family Judge Daniel King turned the forensic battle into a political tug-of-war and directed his wrath solely against me. Just when it appeared that his predecessors had gone bonkers, Judge King took it to a more absurd level, becoming another sadistic ally of the mother. This proved to be especially brazen after I exposed him before the Moreland Commission.

Young Dan King had been on the bench only six months when he was assigned as Judge #35. His shortcomings as a litigation attorney were evident from the moment of our first appearance when he attempted to justify a one-sided order imposed in connection with yet another ex parte petition of the ex. After refusing to hear my side, I requested for the record his rationale. He replied, quite arrogantly, that he was protecting my children. I replied by citing twelve years of childrearing which lacked any finding of unfit parenting. I challenged him to cite anything he knew about my girls, and that no doubt infuriated him to issue spiteful orders that followed.

Among them was an order containing a series of conditions for my weekend parenting time at my niece's wedding where my daughters were set to be flower girls. Ironically, this was initiated by a petition on my part to prevent the custodial parent from concocting a means to preempt that weekend given the cost of dresses already purchased. As it turned out, I became the target once again with conditions that conflicted. My only choice was to violate them which then landed me back in court for contempt.

Since a jail term was a possible outcome, this hearing was serious but conducted during our first appearance without opportunity to bring witnesses. When proofs failed to materialize on either side, Judge King answered with a December 2, 2013 decision suspending my parenting time. Among his grounds was an "alcohol related gesture" (wedding toast) which supposedly violated his prior serial orders. It begs the obvious question: what exactly constitutes such a gesture?

This decision was quickly stayed (stopped) on appeal by Fourth Department Judge John Centra, but it was reimposed by King after a full trial held on January 15, 2014. There I was admonished not to make any more objections to irrelevant testimony of an unrepresented custodial parent under penalty of being removed from the court. There were only five and two were granted, but they were disrupting an orchestrated record to justify earlier orders. Silent and ineffectual with a litany of attacks now aimed at family, I asked and obtained permission to exit. Earlier that month, I spent the last weekend with my girls.

Later that year, Judge King was at it again, this time on more certain grounds of a willful support violation. This is what prompted me to seek protection in Paris. On my return, I retained a friend and counsel during my early ethics case to represent me at yet another hearing on February 10, 2015. The thinking here was that he would mediate the emotions and conclude matters with a sense of finality inasmuch as he had also represented my ex and children indirectly as lawyer for a neighborhood pool club. Mom was a director there and my daughters were members.

Sadly, despite decades of talent and wide respect, all my attorney could do was recommend another agreement which did nothing to change my ongoing loss of valuable parent-child relationships. As King himself emphasized from the bench, he could have put me in jail that very day but was not coercing me to sign an agreement he had personally offered us. It called for a $10,000 payment made that day and $35,500 of remaining support to be paid four months later.

During that period, I discovered by happenstance that the ex had relocated my daughters to her boyfriend's home without notifying me beforehand as required by custody order. She had not disclosed a free residence for a period of eight months on the Family Court record when agreeing to this modified payment arrangement. At the same time, she was collecting rent income on her former home and earning an annual teaching salary close to $100,000 with state benefits.

Logically, therefore, I filed for an order canceling our support agreement based on fraud and a change of custody. King refused to grant immediate relief as he calculated his options. By then, the deadline had lapsed for the balance of support monies due, but I had secured certified bank drafts from friends and relatives in case the standard denials resulted.

Despite the fraud motions pending for argument on September 17, 2015, Family Judge Dan King issued a jail commitment order on September 1, 2015 for willful violation of child support orders with the maximum six months allowed by law. I responded with another stay request which was denied by Fourth Department appeals judge, Nancy Smith, the only jurist above trial level still on the bench punished by the state's Judicial Conduct Commission for ethical misconduct.

Meanwhile my attorney was busy sending King copies of my two certified checks submitted to the state's support collection center. That entity would not reveal its office location in Albany despite its status as a government contractor or agency. That meant that I might have to wait weeks before everything was duly processed while in a fugitive condition.

This delay was exacerbated by King's commitment order which stated that the support violation would be purged (removed) upon payment to the local county support office. The supervisor there informed my agent that they were not authorized to accept my payment. In short, Dan King had issued an order that was impossible to satisfy by its own terms. Even if the later mailed payment to the central office eventually cleared, it would still not comply with King's order.

Consequently, I resorted to state supreme court judge, Anthony Paris, who was presiding at the time over my home foreclosure action. A pending agreement there would guarantee satisfaction of past support as well as future support for the likely duration of my daughters' minor lives with sale proceeds placed in a trust for their benefit. I filed a motion for Judge Paris to order up the King proceedings to his court where his general jurisdiction could legally dispose of all matters.

On September 8, 2015, Judge Paris had me in his chambers on my emergency application for a stay and consolidation of proceedings. He balked at the idea that he could order up the Family Court matter as a trial level jurist. I countered that he could do exactly that under the mandamus provisions of the state civil practice act which I later proved true through an order signed against the same Judge King by another supreme court judge one year later regarding a gag order.

In a sort of compromise, Judge Paris called Judge King at chambers but he had already left for the day. Minutes later, King returned the call on his cell phone. I witnessed the entire exchange although none of the requisite attorneys were notified. Judge Paris convinced King to issue a stay on his own arrest warrant and commitment order set to take effect on 9-11 until September 24, 2015 when "global settlement," as it was called, would be consummated. King consented, and I left the Syracuse courthouse happy for now that I would survive this debacle.

But I knew that Dan King was a Napoleon type, probably kicked around a lot in the school yard. He was not out to benefit anyone's children, our government, its custodial parent or even "F. Lee Billy" Koslosky for that matter. Judge King had re-appointed this child attorney despite his removal from our support case by a prior judge due to his counter-productive involvement.

Without any notice to me or my attorney, Judge King reneged on this arrangement the following day by e-mail to Judge Paris and refused to enter his own stay order. The off-grid nature of all this had me wondering whether King had a private overnight chat with James "Bond" Tormey, his boss. But fate once again intervened when I left on 9-11 eve for a secluded location in Lake Placid just in case.

During the conference with Paris, Judge King offered to decide his stay order on that 9-11 Friday, but Judge Paris interjected that King could also incarcerate me on the spot if he ruled against me. A teleconference became the compromise. But when I received no call by the end of that day, I called Family Court first thing Monday morning to learn that King's arrest warrant had been issued after all. That meant I was already an unknowing fugitive for the past three days.

Now I could be handcuffed and jailed at any highway checkpoint like one which I had survived only two months earlier a few miles west of this Olympic community. I had no plan and no one willing to assist. So I took a giant risk by driving two hours east to Lake George where a friend put me up for the duration of my fugitive period. It just so happened that this friend had recently recorded the most costly two million dollar divorce case in Warren County history.

The drama culminated in a hearing before Judge Paris on September 24, 2015 in my local Oneida County Courthouse. A one day stay was issued by Judge King to facilitate our case consolidation and global settlement proceedings that were being argued in open court that day. I arrived with full knowledge that I could be seized and shackled, coming or leaving, at the courthouse lobby on the good chance that another ambush had been hatched.

The first matter regarding consolidation was decided against me. Technically that meant that jurisdiction over the support warrant remained with King. At that point, a court clerk left for a back room and returned with a sheriff deputy. Certain now that I would be locked in a jail cell for the first time in my crime-free existence, I had to act swiftly, already charting my manner of escape. I had made it clear in court papers that I would treat any King warrant as an abuse of power, an unlawful assault which would justify physical self-defense under our human rights.

It was a life-defining moment, and perhaps the only thing that prevented a horrific ending was a resourceful statement during my argument still underway on the second matter before Judge Paris (global foreclosure settlement). I stated that I would not have been here in good faith if that one day stay by King had not been entered. I'm not sure if Judge Paris picked up on any cues. After all, this was not his courthouse, he was not privy to its politics, but it sure seemed that he did when assuring me from the bench that he was expecting compliance with that stay order.

At that statement, the sheriff deputy left the court room as I did the courthouse shortly afterward with only an open road to Lake George before me, a paradise which had become my eternal home and soulmate. The King orders remained in effect while I was swimming during an unusually extended summer. They were removed only when payment was finally processed.

For weeks, King must have banked on the chance that I would slip up. Instead, I persevered and exposed the clandestine residence relocation excused in an October, 2015 decision denying my fraud motions. I did so through a series of website postings. One month later, King issued a gag order on that website disguised as a protection order. The ex was now claiming that my postings left her, my daughters and her millionaire residential partner in fear of me.

I immediately filed for removal of that gag order on First Amendment grounds. King denied me, and the offense proceedings continued for six needless months with me in limbo over the question of whether all the allegedly offensive postings had been removed from my website. He gave me no clear parameters. The protection order was so vague, overbroad and absurd that it prohibited everything from burglary to "strangulation" of my own daughters!

But that's where the ever oppressive process and gag order backfired. By making the millionaire boyfriend a part of our proceedings, it gave me legal standing to sue him in a mandamus (extraordinary) action before Judge Centra's Fourth Department appeals court. It was quickly dismissed on venue grounds without prejudice to re-file in state supreme court which is what I did. There I was fortunate to get a judge to sign an order against Dan King on May 3, 2016.

Days later, our family offense trial was cancelled after a postponement without explanation. An order was then issued by Judge King dismissing the offense petition and removing the gag order. Significantly, King also vacated a Notice to Admit filed by "F. Lee Billy" Koslosky wherein he tried to legitimize the clearly defective "gmai.com" relocation notice. Although the custodial parent still testified that it transmitted, she retained custody, my parenting suspensions continued, the forensic orders remained without compliance, and the support debacle carried on.

The mandamus action was dismissed as moot when Judge King finally disqualified himself under circumstances suggesting that it was all orchestrated behind the scenes. A protest had been set for June 22, 2016 at the courthouse, the date when King was supposed to defend against my petition. I made sure that the show cause order signed against him was served on him personally as ordered. A deputy sheriff did the honors despite the first copy being accepted by his secretary. After all, King had set the precedent that the law must be strictly observed.

Weeks later, I received a properly noticed e-mail advising that the ex had returned to her former home. In short, she became victim of her own folly. And yet, despite all this, the band played on.

CHAPTER 14

SHOOT ON SIGHT

I was fortunate to get a state supreme court judge to sign the May 3, 2016 order against Judge King's gag order. I was open game by that time given its vagueness and the many website postings that were being scrutinized. Even after I removed all the ones that were conceivably offensive, I could easily have been subjected to contempt by ambush for any violation alleged at a first appearance "mini-trial" as it was called in my case. Then it was off to prison.

But the rights I was exercising comprised much more than free speech. [61] My exposures and reform activity evoked human rights protected by international law. The parenting right existed long before the Magna Charta or American Constitution came to be. It was an inalienable liberty traced to time immemorial, compelling me to file a complaint with the United Nations. I even met with a high ranking member of The Holy See Mission to gain recognition from the Vatican.

While all this was occurring, the mandamus petition I had circulated

---

[61] "The First Amendment reflects a profound national commitment to the principle that debate on public issues should be uninhibited, robust and wide open. This is because speech concerning public affairs is more than self-expression; it is the essence of self-government." Snyder v Phelps, 562 US 443 (2011).

across Paris was making its way to the United States Supreme Court. Among other things, it sought to rectify various abstention practices that lower federal courts had been abusing to dismiss meritorious cases based on federal law violations. [62] Mine was a quintessential example demanding overdue precedent, see also fn. 15. But my petition for writ was denied anyway on October 3, 2016. [63]

In record time, I filed a new petition the very next day taking aim at the people's accessibility rights before our high court. In 1803, it had six members, a nation population of about five million and transportation means limited to horse, foot and water travel. In 2016, the same court had only two more members with a vacancy, a population exceeding 330 million and a complex society that had already put a man on the moon. Expanding its membership was long overdue.

To preserve against political entanglements, my petition (Koziol v King) sought a declaratory opinion by the Supreme Court itself outlining the case for expansion. Some 10,000 petitions are filed each year with only a hundred or so heard. Tremendous talent, resources and trust are evident with their sponsors, but on logistics alone, few petitions are reviewed beyond the 'Questions Presented' page. Highly technical rules require such questions to be placed on a single page following the cover, and any deviation will result in a denial or return for correction.

My hastily prepared petition therefore was focused on that page. Like my "Audacity in Auditing Class" detailed in Chapter Four, I provided much filler for the balance of this particular petition. Its novel approach could be discredited, but then the high court of New York

---

[62] In a trilogy of unanimous opinions, the high court chastised lower courts for such abuses, but the type of case raised here had not yet been reviewed in that context, Sprint Communications v Jacob, 571 US 69 (2013); Marshall v Marshall, 547 US 293 (2006); Exxon Mobile v Saudi Basic Industries, 544 US 280 (2005)

[63] Leon R. Koziol v United States District Court, Supreme Court Docket No. 15-1519 (2016)

could be similarly discredited based on its novel declaratory judgment demanding judicial pay raises. That case was rife with anomalies and jurisdictional irregularities, demonstrating how the law can be twisted to satisfy the pecuniary needs of our courts. [64] My expansion petition was also denied the following month, but it had prophetic relevance to a Supreme Court reform effort five years later, see fn. 1.

This brings us to the year 2017 when another support violation petition was being pursued. It came before yet another support magistrate in Syracuse where I was challenging service of the petition on perjury grounds. A deputy marshal had claimed to serve me with the petition at a local restaurant. In truth, he had approached me in a patron capacity and promised to return with unidentified papers. That never happened, but the deputy signed a contrary sworn statement.

I could have overlooked this, but I was getting furious over the technical rules being rigidly and selectively applied to me. The latest opposing counsel was not present. Instead, he had journeyed to the wrong courthouse when the latest assigned jurist was presiding across the street from his law office. No doubt outraged, his client never made the round trip as the judge took blame for the attorney error. I waited with my key witness for nearly two hours until his belated arrival.

At the hearing, my witness, a former law enforcement officer, testified that he was conducting karaoke at this restaurant and saw my exchange with the deputy but not any transfer of papers. On cross-examination of the deputy, I managed to get his admission to falsifying both the service affidavit and testimony before this very judge. The petition was accordingly dismissed, but no referral was made for perjury charges. So why even bother with the costly service formality?

That question came into sharp focus during the next violation proceeding which was brought in response to my November, 2017

---

[64] Maron v Silver, 14 NY3d 230 (2010)

petition for holiday time with my girls. A seemingly minor service defect ultimately led to a "shoot on sight" threat by a traffic cop on August 30, 2018. It was directed against me and stated to Michael Brancaccio (Chapter Five) who was driving my vehicle with files necessary for an appeal of the later decision. I was fortunately not present.

Two petitions were pending simultaneously. The first regarding holiday time was assigned to Oswego Family Judge James Eby (#37). This was a sadistic jurist with an apparent obsession for provoking me to contempt and a jail term on the spot. He is the one who forced the parties to make a 160 mile round trip to receive a decision that had already been completed. He used that appearance then to lecture me on the correct process for changing a prior custody order, that of taking an appeal which I had successfully completed in numerous cases, see i.e. fn. 68.

On January 4, 2017, in Syracuse, he repeated this lecture for humiliation purposes despite the nonfinal nature of family court orders which precluded any such appeal and the reluctance of appellate courts to intervene. I then asked him to pull out an order from the court file to prove it, that replacement judge decision in 2011 which set aside the Pirro-Bailey forensic orders without an appeal or even a trial. Judge Eby refused my request, instead glaring down at me like a child. I lost two more years of child contact because of this one's ego.

When I arrived at my local family court on December 11, 2017 on our first appearance for holiday time, the custodial parent left the waiting area and visited the nearby court clerk's office. Our case was suddenly called, and while custody issues were still being deliberated upon, a security deputy entered to serve my adversary's support violation petition on me in open court.

The presiding judge Eby stated that this was not policy in his court, but he did nothing to rectify the anomaly despite the deputy acting outside his scope without collecting the prescribed fee. It was obviously orchestrated to prevent a repeat of the last service fiasco, but the overkill proved to be unlawful as the deputy's civil division (with proper service authority) was located only one floor beneath the family court clerk's office. It was sufficient to cause Judge Eby to step down.

This was not a simple act of handing papers to a litigant. That occurs routinely and is often directed by countless judges. This was a defect on jurisdictional grounds with the potential of a criminal act to circumvent legal requirements. Four days later, on the second petition for willful support violation, I raised the same service issue before Judge #40, Natalie Carraway, a newly appointed magistrate. She disregarded it and then angrily denied my motion for disqualification.

Unlike the scheduling issue of the lawyer excused by the prior magistrate, this one failed to call when I missed her next appearance date on the belief that it had been postponed until the preliminary issues before both judges were decided. During this period, I checked out the public warrants list on the Sheriff website to discover my name, set apart from others in capital letters, as a subject of arrest out of support court. Early the next day I called the court to learn of Eby's self-disqualification for the first time and the warrant being signed by his replacement, Utica City Judge Gerald Popeo (#41), assigned by Judge James "Bond" Tormey.

I was outraged on multiple counts and advised the court clerk that I would fight any arrest on this unlawful warrant. But it was lifted hours later on my appearance before Popeo under escort by this same deputy and no arrest. After my exit, I filed for Popeo's removal based on bar talk he initiated six months earlier. He accused me of participating in a "witch hunt" that resulted in his public censure by a judicial commission for racist remarks, threats from the bench and unlawful jail terms.

He was anything but impartial, and all local judges had long refused assignments.

Judge Popeo denied my motion with a lot of calculated script. This then opened the door for a support violation hearing on May 17, 2018 before Magistrate Carraway who, unlike Eby, refused to step down. Somehow, she could not comprehend my position that systemic bias had set in among the serial jurists assigned in the Fifth Judicial District. Like Walsh-Hood earlier, each newly assigned judge was obligated to review the prior record which then disclosed the targeting that was successively joined. Instead of using common sense, Carraway simply piled on.

She also never addressed my retaliation claim on First Amendment grounds, routinely raising her limited jurisdiction as a rationale. However, under well established preclusion rules, my failure to timely raise issues and claims would operate as a waiver even when a limited tribunal was engaged. She could have stayed or postponed her hearing until a competent forum could be secured. My position here was that the judicial branch had effectively suppressed my speech rights through an abuse of lawyer regulations, licensing authority and parens patriae power over children, fn. 4.

This ever-expanding case was undeniably an extraordinary one, and I therefore filed suit in New York Supreme Court to suspend the family court proceedings due to a clear refusal to comply with rights under both federal and state law. In a shocking response, the state attorney general then moved the same case to federal court contrary to its longstanding position in my prior federal filings, namely, that such matters belonged in state court under federal court deference practices.

The assigned federal judge, Glenn Suddaby, accepted the removal and then ruled that my state court filing constituted a scheme to circumvent his earlier conditional, anti-filing order in federal court where I had filed nothing. Again, this really happened. Nevertheless, jumping through the hoops, I filed a petition satisfying his conditions simply to find recourse somewhere for a true scheme of constitutional violations that could be considered racketeering. However, the life-tenured federal judge ruled that my petition was insufficient. In short, one judge effectively appointed himself the gatekeeper to all courts regarding my First and Fourteenth Amendment rights which remain in limbo to the time of this publication.

The extraordinary nature of my case also warranted treatment under a judge-made rule known as "Necessity." This was the rule exploited by New York's high court in the judicial pay raise trilogy, fn. 64. Some judge, somewhere, had to be authorized to hear all my claims in a single court. After fifteen years of judicial ping-pong and misconduct, this rule had long ripened to require a final remedy. It was not my duty to correct a dysfunctional court system. By accepting her assignment and repeatedly denying recusal, that duty fell upon her in the first instance.

In the pay raise trilogy case, the state's judicial branch had taken aim at the other two for the ignoble purpose of increasing salaries through a declaratory judgment against them. Those branches simply treated that judgment as a nullity on grounds of a separation of powers. I had already used this doctrine to invalidate the most lucrative casino compact in New York, fn. 8, but "Naughty Natalie" as we came to call her, was simply raising any excuse to press on with her retaliatory jail objective. No judge is going to admit such misconduct, but the typical way of showing it is through circumstantial proof which was here in abundance.

Again, you be the jury that was never allowed in my fifteen-year ordeal. Young, newly appointed Magistrate Carraway was never vetted for competency by my understanding, and her hearing began with a single witness from Social Services who testified from a reading of agency support summaries. She concluded without any independent knowledge that I was in substantial arrears. Conflicting figures ranged as high as $89,000. However, the support petitioner's attorney rested her client's case without offering the summary into evidence. This made her case woefully inadequate, and I logically moved for dismissal with no reason to put in any defense.

I was forced to do so anyway when my motion was denied, bringing my outrage to new levels. Carraway even emphasized that she could enforce an administrative rule that limited my defense preparation to thirty days between first appearance and this hearing. I then presented a mound of proof showing my inability to obtain employment at age sixty with a public reputation harmed by nearly ten years of driver and law license suspensions.

None of this mattered and after I rested my side of the case, Magistrate Carraway noticed that the support summary had never been offered into the record. She endeavored to accept it belatedly with the Social Services attorney giving quick consent. I interjected with vehement objection since the witness was long gone and I was deprived standard rights of voir dire and cross examination. Carraway then attempted a lame compromise of allowing me to review the summary, however, it had already shown that this particular show trial was fraught with error.

As karma would go, I then discovered that over $45,000 of support payments made in 2015 (Judge King's debacle) had not been credited to me by the agency. This was more than fatal because it implicated a fraud upon the federal government in the way of performance grants based unlawfully on inflated support collections emanating from this hearing. Support Magistrate Carraway then went into damage control. She reversed her decision and handed the summary back to counsel without allowing me a copy.

Despite all this, Naughty Natalie issued a decision recommending that Judge Popeo confirm half the amounts at issue with a maximum jail term of six months. Naturally, I challenged the outcome with a request for stay (postponement) of any confirmation hearing by Popeo to enable procurement of the Carraway transcript and support summary for objection purposes. Standard routine, my request was granted, but a second one was denied thereafter despite two court reporters who mysteriously reneged on their retainers. I never did procure either, and Judge Popeo confirmed the Carraway decision outright conditioned on a purge payment of $46,803.

I was not present at the confirmation hearing because I sensed another ambush, and fortunately so, because when I called in on July 11, 2018, Judge Popeo expressed outrage over my absence, sheriff deputies were waiting, and a false statement was made on the record in another attempt to bury this fiasco. Popeo stated that he would have granted my adjournment request had I appeared in person. I then responded with a prior day e-mail from his court clerk that Popeo was evidently unaware of. That e-mail notified me that Judge Popeo had already denied my second request.

Perhaps enraged, Judge Popeo was not about to step down. Instead he appeared adamant about controlling the outcome while limiting his exposure to judicial misconduct. He issued an arrest warrant and jail term approving Carraway's decision in its entirety. I was already in Queens, New York by then engaged in a campaign against Alexandria Ocasio-Cortez prior to her first election as congresswoman from New York's 14th District. For an entire summer I had become a fugitive resident of New York City awaiting justice upstate which never came.

My two favorite places in the world have always been Lake George and New York City, polar opposites from every imaginable dimension. During the "shoot-on-sight" period, my second home became the Sheraton Four Points in Long Island City where a friendly staff took good care of me. Its rates were half of those charged on the other side of the nearby Queensboro

Bridge. Astoria became my neighborhood, and I regularly got my breakfasts and dinners at the outdoor cafes along Ditmars Boulevard. McCanns and Rocky McBrides were my late night hang-outs.

Queens is a fascinating place. It boasts the most diverse population in the world. As the largest borough, it could easily qualify as the fifth or sixth largest city in the United States especially when counting the residents who were undocumented. For the most part, it had retained family values and a work ethic that reminded me of a time when I was very young. I met a lot of interesting people in Queens, too many to relate fairly in a book. To know it was to live there, and this was when I finally got that opportunity of a lifetime.

But my love of the Big Apple was always entrenched in Manhattan. Prior to my first visit at age sixteen, I had already memorized its attractions, demographics and lay-out. As an appellate lawyer, I argued cases before the federal appeals court at Foley Square. Later on, my reform activity would expand my presence among the many neighborhoods there, mini-cities if you will. They included Hell's Kitchen, Greenwich Village, Chelsea, Little Italy and East Village.

In 2015, I managed to attract the interest of a high profile doctor suffering through his own ordeal as a divorce litigant. After spending more than $5 million on lawyer fees alone, he was now committed to vengeance in the way of reform. I became his ideal advocate, invited to monitor his family court proceedings for purposes of exposing corruption. He even gave me a bedroom in his luxury, high-rise apartment in Tribeca where I got to know lower Manhattan. Now how often does one get that opportunity at no cost?

Prior to the time of my reform activity, I took my daughters to Manhattan for the Macy's Day Parade. Aged six and seven at the time, I feared that they could easily become overwhelmed by all the congestion, fast pace and culture shock. But like a chip off the old block, they were enthralled by everything they came across. It was holiday time in the city that never sleeps, so they were able to experience all the ambiance at Rockefeller Center.

Together with my girlfriend I took them on a carriage ride through Times Square. At Central Park the next day they were treated to countless forms of free entertainment. A lone saxophone player got their attention first, and he was not doing well with donations. With festive pink dresses on, my girls looked like twins as they showed off their dance moves, pirouetting to a growing crowd. By the time they were done with their own spontaneous act, the sax player could not thank them enough for his take.

Shortly after Popeo's warrant issued, the security deputy contacted me by phone to offer a repeat of our arrangement six months earlier, that of paying the purge amount in person at the courthouse without formal arrest. After the King, Carraway and Popeo debacles, however, I could not trust anyone now. I replied that I would again fight this warrant which was my right under these extremes. I also reminded him of the judicial misconduct and the deputy's own complicity which caused this whole fiasco in the first place. Then I hung up.

This obviously offended him personally because a selectively crafted bulletin followed with none of the misconduct mentioned during the call. This deputy's boss, Oneida County Sheriff Robert Maciol, admitted publicly that this secret bulletin had been unlawfully leaked, but my prior conduct complaints regarding that deputy received not so much as a generic acknowledgment from him. This was no small matter as domestic violence incidents were erupting in his county. Another deputy had been killed in one such incident under Maciol's watch.

Former client and support victim Michael Brancaccio needed a new life, so I added him to our campaign staff in New York. On August 30, 2018, he was delivering bagged files in my vehicle needed for appeal of the Popeo outcome. Prior to his arrival, I received a highly agitated call from Mike informing me that his three hour tardiness was justified by events he could not disclose at his location on Interstate 87 in Albany, New York. When we finally made contact in person, he advised of a multi-agency stop and interrogation based on that secret bulletin.

Apparently, my license plate had been pinged at the toll booths minutes before his detainment. The several agencies were demanding that he take them to my location based on a bulletin containing website and Facebook photos of my buffed-up physical condition which was put in Mike's face. The first of two was taken at a beach in Hawaii where I had been retained to write an autobiography for a persecuted mom three years earlier. The second was a February, 2017 photo taken in Central Park to prove weather conditions in the seventies.

There was simply too much law enforcement applied to this child support warrant while terrorists, drug smugglers and dangerous fugitives were driving by this same traffic stop. But this was the extreme to which my adversaries had taken to effectively end my life. I had no criminal record, violent disposition or weapons registered to me. When Mike resisted all threats, a local cop stated that "we shoot on sight" when enforcing such warrants.

Upon learning of the imminent nature of this shocking threat in New York City, I nearly dropped unconscious to the floor. I had been reduced to target practice much like my dad had been in Nazi Germany or our patriots during the Revolutionary War. Even my closest friends were keeping their distance to avoid charges of assisting a fugitive after this bulletin was leaked.

For the next six weeks, I feared for my life each time an NYPD car showed up in my vicinity. It was a harrowing period which fortunately I survived once the purge payments were processed. After that, I focused my energies on petitioning Congress to hold public hearings on the abuses of Title IV-D funding. I again sought a comprehensive investigation of my ordeal by the Justice Department which I compared to Operation Greylord. That federal sting operation resulted in the convictions of nearly one hundred judges, lawyers and officials in Chicago during the 1980s.

To garner public support for both the hearings and investigation, I sponsored a three-day event at our nation's capital in May, 2019. I called it the Parent March on Washington. This was no small task on a donated budget of under $500. But it was well attended by parent victims from across the country and featured a lobby day in Congress, an expert speakers event at a hotel ballroom, a march down Pennsylvania Avenue under police escort, and a candlelight vigil at the Capitol to memorialize all the tragic victims of this family court system.

Our New York contingent filled the conference room of Senator Chuck Schumer, but no responses came of any of this, causing participants to rightfully conclude that peaceful protests were ineffectual. George Floyd activists made the same pitch one year later to justify volatile protests across the country. More alarming, despite my exposure of this "shoot on sight" event in a report to members of Congress, no mention of it was made. Its genuine occurrence was backed by affidavit and tape recording while I scrutinized the demeanor of Michael Brancaccio using my trial skills. I did this not so much for proof reasons but because my very life could be in peril.

Even in litigation before trial, a judge will single out such an allegation in chambers or on the record. After all, given the growing number of police cover-ups being exposed nationwide, any jurist sworn to uphold the Constitution will express concern of some kind. In my experience I had seen much more concern for debt collections known as child support. But no federal, state or appellate judge appeared moved by this event detailed in court papers, the kind of summary killing historically associated with tyrannical regimes. Now that is scary, I mean real scary.

EPILOGUE

As a civil rights attorney, I spent over two decades litigating for victims of race, gender, religion and ethnic discrimination. This included sexual harassment cases when they were unpopular. Many successful verdicts, monetary recoveries and precedent outcomes resulted. But my crusade for justice was not limited to minorities. It also extended to white landowners wrongfully threatened with eviction in the Oneida Indian land claim. Police brutality cases were similarly prosecuted for diverse victims, and I represented a public safety commissioner, police chief and rank and file officers whenever they were falsely accused.

In short, I was motivated to correct injustices to a point where I managed to have a billion-dollar casino compact invalidated on constitutional grounds in New York Supreme Court. The Las Vegas Sun reported it as a David-Goliath battle won by "the small Utica law firm that won the case." [65]Among the defense firms was Cravath, Swaine and Moore, one of the most powerful in the nation. These achievements earned me praise from federal and state judges. The court transcripts, headline news and published opinions bear this out.

However, when I turned my energies to correcting human rights violations in divorce and family courts, I was viciously targeted. Suddenly, my arguments were incomprehensible, rambling and frivolous

---

[65] Michael Gormley, *Judge strikes down pact,* Las Vegas Sun, June 29, 2004. Peterman v Pataki, 2004 Slip. Op. 51092. The final judgment was affirmed on appeal.

after twenty-three unblemished years. Even I underestimated the wrath of a corrupt regime bent on retaliation for my exposure of corruption involving a judge-lawyer gold mine. In numerous public statements, I cited federal funding abuses and lucrative custody battles that were inciting child murders, veteran suicides and needless parental conflict.

As a consequentially victimized parent, I was then forced to assume the mantra of a judicial whistleblower devoid of legal protection. The horrific ordeal here remains unprecedented in modern times. Among the practices I condemned in chapter two and an earlier book, *Satan's Docket*, was the abuse of forensic custody evaluations. Then, in January, 2022, a blue-ribbon panel appointed by New York's governor voted to eliminate these evaluations altogether. I made a presentation at a virtual public hearing sponsored by that panel asking for this very outcome, but like the Moreland Commission on Public Corruption (where I also appeared), it is doubtful that any genuine reform will be implemented. That is how powerful this gold mine has become.

So, in the spirit of Dr. Martin Luther King, I sponsored a three-day event at our nation's capital in May, 2019. Its goal was to elicit a Justice Department investigation and congressional hearings into the rampant human rights violations and federal funding abuses which continue to be ignored in these custody and support courts. We featured planning sessions, a lobby day among the offices of Congress, expert speakers at a hotel ballroom, a candlelight vigil in front of the U.S. Capitol, and a march down Pennsylvania Avenue under police escort from the White House to the Supreme Court.

All of this was accomplished without incident on a shoestring budget. At least four necessary permits were obtained together with regulatory compliance. Parents came from all parts of the country to register their peaceful protest against divorce and family court corruption. Yet not a single member of Congress responded. Then-president Donald Trump never materialized in front of the crowd assembled at the White House. Not even a representative was sent. The Justice Department weighed in with the same message that parental rights were not even on their radar. His successor, Joe Biden, proved oblivious to this crisis altogether.

So what is the lesson to be realized from all this? Peaceful protests to benefit parents, children and families of all races, religions and ethnic backgrounds will be ignored. They yield no respect whatsoever while the same politicians beg for our support on election day through such things as a voting rights bill. Therefore, it is time for those struggling against parental alienation, custody abuses and support debtor prisons to take matters into their own hands. Stay away from lawyers and these courts, set aside your custody and support disputes, and keep abreast of fellow victims who need your help. In this way at least, we might succeed in closing the gold mine.

Thinking back to all the craziness I endured for more than a decade under the yoke of this antiquated child custody regime, it still amazes me that not a single inquiry was made by the New York Commission on Judicial Conduct regarding the many complaints I lodged. How could so much corruption become so buried? I am also amazed at all the physical restraint I practiced. Under our form of government, when the courts break down, victims can seek recourse outside the system. Nevertheless, my restraint led to poetic justice in so many ways.

Among the Sadistic Seven, Michael Daley is no longer a judge, having failed to garner enough support for re-election to the bench. His unpopularity was borne out later when he was defeated in an election for his old job as a local prosecutor. Last I heard he was representing traffic clients in Utica city court.

Judge Martha Walsh-Hood continues to serve as a family court judge as does her colleague Michele Pirro-Bailey in Syracuse. Judge Daniel King is still on the family court bench in Lowville, New York, but is up for re-election in 2022. At a minimum, my whistleblower testimony before the Moreland Commission on Public Corruption should be raised by any opposing candidate. The judge collusion inferred by King's sudden removal of his gag order during my mandamus action in state Supreme Court remains a part of the public record. The manner in which this was all arranged behind closed doors demands a proper investigation.

Regardless, not one of these judges was elevated to higher office. This includes Judge James Eby who no longer presides over my case in Oswego, New York. In the aftermath of his uncorrected bias, innocent third parties were irreparably harmed. During his bombastic antics directed at me, he gave no concern for extended family similarly denied all contact with my daughters. He simply pressed on with his ego-driven agenda of retaliation to maintain favor among colleagues on and off the bench.

To be sure, as director of the Parenting Rights Institute, I continue to receive complaints about him, one from a custodial mother regarding his knack for keeping the fees coming. He makes a mockery of this self-serving rationale of acting "in the best interests" of our children whose basic needs and college funds are raided. Entire families are bankrupted in the process while inciting domestic violence. An adversarial process rationalized by truth-seeking objectives cannot withstand the ultimate injury it yields when children are placed at needless risk compelling parents to resort to uncharacteristic extremes to protect them.

Similarly, Judge Gerald Popeo in Utica is also no longer presiding. He declined re-election prospects following my crusade against him in 2018. The judge censure which he blamed partly on me no doubt played a role in his decision. Magistrate Natalie Carraway continues her routine in support courts of Herkimer County, presumably charting a course for higher judgeship. Meanwhile, I continue to receive unsolicited praise from countless parents who publicly credit me for private changes in attitude among certain well-meaning jurists.

But it may also be said that poetic justice was served beyond the Sadistic Seven. My pedophile custody judge, Bryan Hedges, was permanently banned from the bench by the high court of New York, his colleague in Syracuse, Michael Hanuszczak, was forced to step down for sexual harassment of his court clerks, and Magistrate G. Stephen Getman lost an election for family court judge. His license suspension for mishandling client money caught up to him in that race.

My ex-secretary was jailed for crimes upon later victims. Her scheme with outsiders to orchestrate ethics issues in my office together with her tampering of mail and files resulted in the removal of a $220,000 mortgage claim on my home. It is unlikely that she will ever be hired for another law-related position given her felony convictions and our creation of a pretend lawyer website that features her. She would not have contemplated such crimes unless cloaked with some concealed protection while my office supervision was derailed by the family court battles.

My ex-wife was removed from the millionaire's home in 2016 after wasting untold resources to pursue a needless parent alienation campaign bent on greed, revenge and jealousy. She too could not have succeeded without the undisclosed backing of many of the judges assigned to our case. But this particular campaign exceeded the worst I have come across. It can only be described as something hatched out of hell itself, a new form of evil. It harmed not only her children and their father but it devastated her own world. Yet she pressed on like the proverbial energizer bunny.

You would think that this "custodial parent" learned a profound lesson when her relocation scheme to that millionaire's home was exposed. It featured the "gmai.com" concoction which she and the child attorney tried to pass as proper notice of a new residency. At a minimum, a parent has a right to know where his or her children are residing and with whom so that they can be better safeguarded. But here, despite undeniable proof of deceit upon the father, court and schools, this scheme was accorded no accountability in contrast with money obligations (child support) which were hounded to a point of arrest warrants, jail commitments and even death.

This one-sided persecution had no effect on her commitment to forever end all father-daughter relationships developed since birth. In August, 2021, the newly married Kelly Usherwood contrived an exit from the region on the day after my youngest daughter's eighteenth birthday. She placed her home on the market and relocated both my girls to an undisclosed residence without even an identity of colleges they were now attending. By text message, she directed that any information was to be exchanged through the maternal grandmother nearby.

As fate would have it, this grandmother deceased only three months later. Meanwhile, circumstances showed that the e-mail exchanges made between father and his daughters were actually being made by the mother. This is how devious the alienator had become to achieve her objective of a family unit completely isolated from the biological father, one who had never even been found to be an unfit parent. It proved to be spite, greed and status which motivated Kelly Usherwood to pursue the unimaginable while the band played on in these corrupt family courts.

None of this should surprise the reader given the content of earlier chapters and the growing horrors of parental alienation throughout the country. The unilateral directives of this deranged mother comported with no court order, but with the long confirmed systemic bias among numerous assigned judges in New York's Fifth Judicial District, and the deference repeatedly given them by federal court, all courthouse doors had been closed in terms of any civil recourse. If Daniel King could invent a "prohibited alcohol related gesture" (wedding toast) as a reason to suspend child contact, how could I expect any sanity from the judges who replaced him?

The recent concealment of my daughters raises concerns that could warrant an amber alert given the bizarre conduct of the alienator-abductor. It occurred in the aftermath of my extended hospital stay only months earlier. Despite a life-threatening condition, no direct contact was received from my daughters. By the time the realities of brainwashing caught up to them, it would be too late to revisit countless precious moments captured in home videos and photos.

In the end, it begs the question: what kind of evil lurks in the body of Kelly Usherwood? The answer may lie in some sequel of American Greed or a psycho movie. Even my girls were not spared the karma behind their immoral disregard of dad during his hospital stay, the man who made their existence possible. Both daughters were forced to suffer through a pandemic which is continuing. Graduations, proms and other once-in-a-lifetime events were either canceled or subjected to highly diluting regulations.

As for the ethics lawyers who helped facilitate this chaos, they were forced to resign after an investigation into falsified time sheets. Would-be clients continue to be denied qualified representation. Even after eleven years of license suspension, I continue to receive calls from victims who cannot secure basic legal advice. The system justified this by support obligations that cannot be satisfied without the licenses, resources and liberties that were seized.

This so-called disciplinary process was abused to achieve censorship, thereby making its perpetrators complicit in the resulting crimes upon humanity. Despite all this, corruption was exposed on a vast scale after unprecedented numbers of jurists were removed from my originally uncontested divorce. Those removals helped alter the divorce culture in a positive way while exposing the underbelly of a court system hell-bent on revenues and profits.

But I paid a high price. Out of law school in 1987, I was able to secure a restraining order on a $30 million high school project, [66] I won my first interstate divorce appeal two years later, [67] my name appears on two dedication plagues of the Utica city courthouse as an elected councilman and corporation counsel, I was a featured speaker regarding Native American land claims across upstate New York, and I won a $300,000 civil rights recovery against my local Sheriff which may have factored into the later antics. Other high-profile cases are cited at footnotes 7-11.

Today I am unable to get a family judge to order phone contact with my own daughters.

In raw terms, you can kill a targeted person with a gun or accomplish the same outcome with a drawn-out process that chips away at your existence. Parent alienation is such a process. It is more than a psychological syndrome or human rights violation, it is a proven killer of victimized parents. Whether it be a suicide, terminal illness or some other brutal consequence, the needless separation of a loving parent from his or her children is simply unconscionable. And when forcing the victim to pay for the child abduction through support payments under penalty of a debtor prison, it becomes utterly barbaric.

Judges are quick to overlook this reality as they routinely find breaches of various duties in personal injury cases to achieve million-dollar verdicts. But when greater breaches of ethical duties are presented regarding their own conduct, they cloak themselves with judicial immunity on the rationale that such liability would deter qualified candidates from

---

[66] In Rome Concerns Citizens v Rome City School District, this restraining order made possible a state-of-the art high school now located at the Griffiss Technology Park. As fate would go, a base realignment commission led to the closure of the former Griffiss Air Force Base after my controversial litigation. It was the region's top employer. A tech park became its replacement which benefits faculty and students in a myriad of ways today. The former proposed school location could not have facilitated such benefits due to remoteness and land constraints.

[67] DeNigro v DeNigro, 152 AD2d 951 (4th Dept 1989)

seeking judgeships. Utter nonsense, most lawyers crave these prestigious titles, and a judge complying with job requirements has nothing to fear. If anything, this absolute immunity encourages misconduct while politically-appointed oversight commissions fail us time and again.

This ordeal warrants a Justice Department investigation and congressional inquiry. It would benefit countless moms, dads and families similarly situated. There are tremors of unrest throughout this country which are being ignored. Hardly a day goes by without some child murder, needless suicide or unpredictable homicide traced to these dysfunctional courts. What remains of a stable society is largely made possible by the free exercise of parental liberties and self-governance. It is my fervent hope, therefore, that a powerful movement emerges from my sacrifices that forces our government to pay attention to its own parents.

This literary work is by no means an indictment of our justice system or legal profession. However, it verifies in painstaking detail how a conscientious attorney, model parent and judicial whistleblower can be so ruthlessly punished for his crusade to deliver overdue reforms to our system of family court justice. The people rely on qualified insiders to alert them to corruption in our third branch of government. It accentuates the need for attorney whistleblower protection.

Finally, this book is directed against the divorce industry and the family court predators who are dragging justice down to hell, a people's courthouse reduced to a giant profit center. All this corruption might compel another victim to resort to violence. But I was able to forbear it and achieve some justice in more constructive ways. My old friend, Sir Walter Scott, gave me sage advice in that regard:

> *For he that does good, having the unlimited power to do evil, deserves praise not only for the good he performs, but the evil he forbears.*

Printed in the United States
by Baker & Taylor Publisher Services